The Fifth

GLO'STER

GAZETTE

This edition selected, arranged and published in 2013 by Anne Crow
annecrow@hotmail.co.uk
Copyright © Anne Crow

Cover design overleaf drawn in 1915 by
Second Lieutenant K. Robertson, M.C.

Selected Contributions from

The Fifth Glo'ster Gazette 1915 - 1919

"A Chronicle, serious and humorous, of the Battalion while serving with the British Expeditionary Force"

Compiled, arranged and edited by Anne Crow

In 1922, all twenty-five issues of the *Gazette*, the very first trench newspaper, were re-published with the following Preface:

Preface

The decision of re-publishing the *Gloucester Gazette* in book form is a good one. It will stand out and remain for long years a Memento of the Great War, and find a place on the bookshelf of many members of the 1/5th Battalion Gloucester Regiment, be he Officer, Non-Commissioned Officer or man of that Battalion.

The Fifth Gloucester Gazette will keep green the memory of many a hard day, weary month and still longer years of those who fought and endured so splendidly for the cause of freedom. It was a wonderful, a brilliant thought, to publish a Magazine even in the very face of the enemy. It showed the spirit of our men, who could raise a laugh and smile when shells, mines and bombs were exploding around them. And yet not only jests or a gibe at some mannerism or peculiarity of certain persons may be found among its pages, but some really good poems, some deeply religious thought poetically expressed are of frequent occurrence.

The *Gloucester Gazette* will, therefore, be an interesting character study, for it shows that, although a man may laugh, even when surrounded by death and destruction, there is also another side to our soldier's character, whether it be called sentimental, poetic, or religious, which shows itself in the long hours of duty, or in the dullness of the Rest Camp, where he is thinking of home, his family or his native land.

A. B. BATHURST, Colonel (1922)

List of written contributions

Introduction (1922)

It happened in the early days of April, 1915, that, after a serious bout of deep depression and nervous apprehension at Chelmsford (I suppose that one may now be permitted to say where the Battalion was in training), Lieutenant-Colonel Collett first launched the idea of publishing a Battalion Gazette, whilst some of us were sitting round the fire in a small farmhouse hard by what was then the pleasant little village of Meteren. He offered a prize for the best design for the cover. This was awarded to Second-Lieut. K. Robertson, MC, then a Private in 'C' Company, and, from our rest billets at Romarin, the design was despatched to Mr. John Jennings of Gloucester for execution.

The first two numbers were laboriously typed and duplicated by Private Pyne, who, fortunately for us, was serving as a Brigade Clerk, and therefore gifted with a fairly reasonable amount of access to stores of paper, more or less 'uncontrolled'. He will pardon our frank admission that one issue, through no fault of his, partook somewhat of the nature of a Missing Letter and Mangled Word Competition. For it will readily be conceded that a disused and dirty Franco-Belgian farmhouse attic, half of which was in Belgium and half in France, was no ideal birthplace for a great newspaper. Nevertheless, "the midnight mouse and the peeping stars marvelled as, hour after hour, the staff – note the small 's' please - covered themselves with imperishable glory and their hands with indelible ink."

Number Three was printed in a little printing press that once looked out on to the noble square of Bailleul, but was only ready for distribution when the Battalion had moved away from 'Plug Street', and was in rest in the golden village of

Allouagne. Henceforth, till August, 1917, when, owing to the difficulties of transport, recourse was had to sending off the 'copy' to Gloucester, the *GAZETTE* was published at Amiens. As the printers of that fair city knew no English, and the Editor was equally ignorant of decent French, proof-correcting was no easy matter. Thus the first proof of, say, a football match resembled a message in code more than anything else. However, by means of patience on the part of the printers and blandishments on the part of the Editor, through the kindness of No. 4 Company train and the O.C.'s of three Field Ambulances, *GAZETTES* appeared from time to time with a perfectly consistent irregularity.

It is no exaggeration to say that the *GAZETTE,* thanks to the ability of a few contributors, was a success from the very start. In the world of letters, Bishop Frodsham and Mr. E.B. Osborne, of the *Morning Post,* to both of whom the *GAZETTE* owes much, were quick to recognise the genius of Lieut. F.W. Harvey, DCM, at that time a Lance-Corporal in 'C' Company. His wealth of imagery, so homely in its hunger for the Malvern Hills, so original in treatment of the commonplace, marked him out as a poet of no mean order.

It was very largely due to his efforts that the *GAZETTE* survived the very difficult days of its infancy. Lieut. Cyril Winterbotham, who was killed in the very hour of victory, on Sunday August 27th, after being the first to reach the objective, and himself shooting the Hun sentry, had only the previous day handed me those immortal lines on *'The Wooden Cross',* lines which very truly served as his own epitaph. His contributions in lighter vein were always subtle and arresting in their humour. The initials 'H.S.K.' and in a lesser degree 'G.F.C.' – we refer to the quantity, not to the quality – were to be found beneath compositions which shewed their owners to be possessed of some very pungent wit. Their barbed shafts had a way of 'getting home'.

As time went on, contributions would come in from other units, chief among whom were Captain W.O. Down, MC, a skilled playwright of repute with a great future before him, killed near Demicourt, and Captain James, MC, both of whom were serving with the 4th Royal Berks. When they collaborated, the one with his pen the other with his pencil, the results were particularly happy. Captain Down's dainty verse and clever parody were alike instinct with charm and grace. Lieut. Gedye, of the Bristol R.F.A. ('Emma Kew'), a real humorist, was killed in a gallant attempt to extinguish a dump on fire at Crucifix Corner. The death of Major Pridmore, MC, R.F.A., was another great loss to the *GAZETTE*.

The retirement of 'C.S.N.' and 'F.R.B.' of our own Battalion, to England, with wounds, was the means of depriving us of two very valuable contributors. Meanwhile, Capt. G. Hawkins perpetrated a large amount of genuine wit, his parody on '*Good King Wenceslas*' being very daring, and as a writer of Dud Orders, he has few equals. It was due to him and to Captain R.F. Rubinstein ('Fibulous') that the gaiety of the letterpress was, at any rate, preserved, if not enhanced, whilst Lieut. Robertson, MC, as often as not, under the pseudonym of 'Owl', provided a series of amusing drawings. Writing in a more serious vein, 'M.L.G.' shewed a wealth of imagination and the command of a lucid style, a somewhat rare and, therefore, treasured combination.

But it is already high time that this introduction came to a speedy close. Yet it would be ungracious not to emphasise the debt that is owing to the little band of writers who did so much towards the maintenance of a jolly spirit in the Battalion, whether it was engaged in keeping clear the *Pas de tir*, waiting at Couin as zero hour on July 1st, 1916, approached, or in whiling away the time at Le Sars, R.3, St. Julien, or on the Italian Front. Not a few of those who gladdened us with their jokes, poems and articles now sleep the long sleep, some hard by the Happy Valley on the Somme, others on the dull flats of Flanders, others again amid the pine trees of Asiago. But they helped to victory almost as much with their pens as they did with their rifles, for the tramp of tired feet has oftentimes been quickened by their ready wit, and the mud and misery forgotten once again.

> "Rest ye content. More honourable far
> Than all the Orders is the Cross of Wood,
> The symbol of self-sacrifice which stood
> Bearing the God whose brethren ye are."

By Padre G.F. Helm (1922)

Introduction (2013)

In March 1915, the Fifth Battalion of the Gloucestershire Regiment, their ranks swollen with thousands of volunteers, sailed to France to take their place at the Western Front. Seeking to raise the morale of his troops, the Commanding Officer, Lt-Col. Collett, launched the very first British regimental trench journal, *The Fifth Gloucester Gazette,* which sold for 3d a copy. The editor was the regimental Chaplain, Padre George Francis Helm, who stayed with the Battalion until August, 1917.

The Padre was determined that the *Gazette* would be written by serving soldiers of all ranks, so he set about persuading the men to give him poems, sketches, stories, cartoons or whatever they wished to submit. In the first issue he invited contributions, certain that "many men will be anxious to contribute to a Gazette which will record the sayings and doings, the tears and smiles of Gloucestershire men." The *Gazette* gave them the opportunity to voice their feelings, anonymously if they so wished. There were 25 issues of the *Gazette,* printed between April 1915 and January 1919, and they are remarkable for the insight they give into the comradeship which helped them to face their ordeal with resignation and laughter, and to tackle their task with determination.

There were regular items such as reports of casualties, promotions, results of friendly sports matches, and also facetious columns such as *'What we want to know'*. This book contains only a few of the contributions, selected because they speak to a modern audience. The army slang and technical terms are explained in a glossary at the back of this book. Some contributions were anonymous, but, where possible, names or initials have been included.

Anne Crow

EVOLUTION.

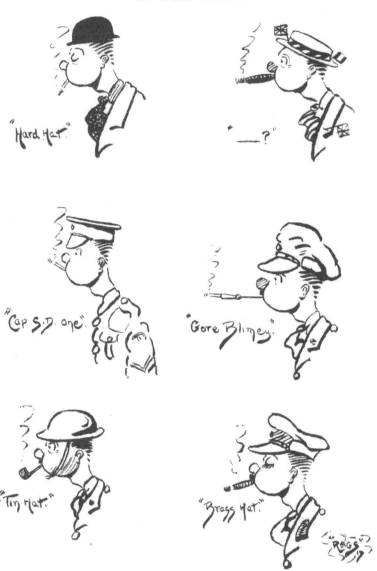

The following light-hearted poem shows how the editor chivvied contributions out of men who would never have written voluntarily, but eventually welcomed the opportunity to express their views and to have fun while they did it:

Jarge's Poem (by 'Y')
(George's Poem, to be read in a Gloucestershire accent)

The young gent who edits this blooming Gazette
      Said to I just a day back, or two,
"Jarge, I take it as lucky as you and I met,
      For I'd like to have something from you."

"Right you are, Sir," says I, "wot be yours, beer or stout?
      I don't mind for myself which you name.
In this 'ere blighting country to which we've come out
      I can ne'er get enough of that same."

But the young gent, says he, with a very broad grin,
      "Jarge, my meaning I fear you've mistook.
I said 'from' you, not 'with', and I want you to spin
      Me a poem or yarn for my book."

Then I laughed till the tears washed my beautiful face
      As it ain't 'a bin washed for a week.
An' my ribs ached as if they'd gone out of their place
      An' 'ad slipped back again with a creak.

Says I, "Sir, you ain't asking much, I don't think,
      From a bloke which 'is real job is fightin',
I don't say as 'ow I ain't good at a drink,
      But I ain't any good, Sir, at writin'.

And yet, Sir," says I, "I often do feel
    That if only I COULD write a story,
I'd tell 'em such tales of these chaps true as steel
    Who are out here a fightin' for glory

As would make the folks 'ome 'ardly know which to do
    'Eave their chests out with pride, Sir, or cry.
For I know what 'eroes my pals are, and you
    Know that too, Sir, the same just as I.

You know as it ain't any picnic we're at.
    You've been in the trenches like me,
An' you've seen my pals bleeding and dying; and that
    Ain't the pleasantest sight you can see.

You've seen 'ow we stands facin' death night an' day,
    An' those slackers at 'ome, I could show 'em,
If only I COULD say all I could say
    In the style of a yarn or a poem.

But you, why don't YOU, Sir, write home and just say
    'Ow we need every man who is fit.
An' the chaps must come out an' take part in the play
    An' not watch other chaps do their bit.

If they're too old to fight, Sir, or can't pass the Doc,
    Let them stay an' make shells, Sir, or guns,
Then we'll give Kaiser Bill such a 'ell of a shock –
    - 'Ow I 'ates Kaiser Bill an' 'is 'Uns!

If I had a few of 'em 'ere by the neck
    In that dirty old 'orse-pond I'd throw 'em,
But lor, Sir, it's time as I passed in my check,
    An' I'm blowed if I ain't writ a poem!"

Throughout the *Gazette,* these themes are repeated: respect and admiration for their pals in the regiment, contempt for those who have not joined up, and the poignant understatement of the terrible sights they have witnessed.

The soldiers of the Fifth Gloucestershire Regiment shared a love for their home county, beautifully expressed here by Lance-Corporal (later Lieut.) F.W. Harvey D.C.M. Harvey was decorated for bravery in the field, but, in August 1916, he was captured by the Germans from behind their lines. He was taken to the P.O.W. camp of Gütesloh, the first of seven prison camps he was to endure. He managed to send poems home: two books were published, and reviewed in the *Gazette.* In reviewing these books, the *Cheltenham Chronicle* dubbed him "The Laureate of Gloucestershire".

A Gloucestershire Wish

Here's luck, my lads, while Birdlip Hill is steep:
As long as Cotteswold's high, or Severn's deep,
Our thoughts of you shall blossom and abide
While blow the orchards about Severn side.

While a round bubble like the children blow
May Hill floats purple in the sunset glow.
Our prayers go up to bless you where you lie
While Gloucester town stands up against the sky.

To write old thoughts of loveliness and trace
Dead men's long living will to give God praise
Who of His mercy doth His own son give
This blessed morn that you and all may live.

F.W.H.

In Flanders

I'm homesick for my hills again --
  My hills again!
To see above the Severn plain
Unscabbarded against the sky
The blue high blade of Cotswold lie;
The giant clouds go royally
By jagged Malvern with a train
Of shadows. Where the land is low
Like a huge imprisoning O
I hear a heart that's sound and high,
I hear the heart within me cry –
"I'm homesick for my hills again --
  My hills again!
Cotswold, or Malvern, sun or rain!
  My hills again." F.W.H.

Not all of Harvey's poems find escape in romantic nostalgia.

To the Kaiser – confidentially

I met a man – a refugee -
  And he was blind in both his eyes, Sir,
And in his pate
  A silver plate
('twas rather comical to see!)
  Shone where the bone skull used to be
Before your shrapnel struck him, Kaiser,
  Shattering in the self-same blast
(Blind as a tyrant in his dotage)
  The foolish wife
Who risked her life,
  As peasants will do to the last,
Clinging to one small Belgian cottage.

That was their home. The whining child
    Beside him in the railway carriage
Was born there, and
    The little land
Around it (now untilled and wild)
    Was brought him by his wife on marriage.
The child was whining for its mother,
    And interrupting half he said, Sir,
I'll never see the pair again,
    Nor they the mother that lies dead, Sir.

That's all – a foolish tale, not worth
    The ear of noble lord or Kaiser,
A man un-named,
    By shrapnel maimed,
Wife slain, home levelled to the earth,
    That's all. You see no point? Nor I, Sir.
Yet on the day you come to die, Sir,
    When all your war dreams cease to be,
Perchance will rise
    Before your eyes
(Piercing your hollow heart, Sir Kaiser!)
    The Picture that I chanced to see
Riding (we'll say) from A to B.   F.W.H.

The Battalion A.B.C. (excerpt)

E. is for England, now distant and dear,
   When we see her white cliffs again, how we will cheer.
F. is the Frenchman who answered "Quite so"
   To our "S'il vous plaît Monsieur, donnez-moi l'eau."
G. is the Glo'sters – those grim, gory fighters
   Who've cleared all the trenches from Bailleul to Ypres.
                            F.W.H.

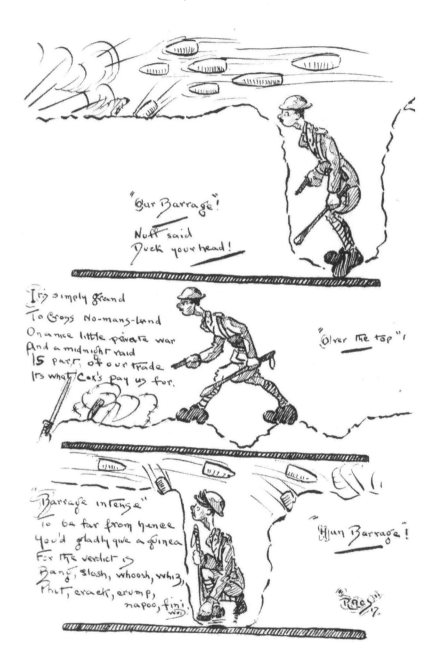

Victory

Whether you shall see it, or I,
We cannot tell
Now. And it doesn't matter.

For 'twill come when Hell
Is covered, and the batter
Of guns fades: -- Victory!

Remember this, you who have followed the dead
Through the worst, loudest, last
Thunder before the sun –

Remember – Though the Hun
And his brute power has passed –
There are more wars to be won!

O, while Life's Life to all eternity: --
Brothers press on, GO ON TO VICTORY!   F.W.H.

In Memoriam

Why should we mourn the dead (since death
Will come to everyone)
Who go in valiant youth, and yet
Unspoiled with life and living's fret,
While still the seasons run
Ever more wearily and weak for him who tarrieth?

They never crept into the night
That lurks for all mankind.
Joyous they lived, and joyous leapt
Into the gaping dark where slept
Their fathers all: to find
Honour, the jest of fools, yet still the soul of all delight.

                    F.W.H.

Casualties

"No easy hopes or lies
Shall bring us to our goal,
But iron sacrifice
    Of Body, Will and Soul.
There is but one rank for all
For each one life to give.
Who stands if Freedom fall?
Who dies if England live?"

Sometimes the contributors made up new lyrics to be sung to familiar tunes, like this song, in which the bouncy tune of *'Roaming in the Gloaming'* helps to make light of their fears.

'The Song of the Reconnoitring Patrol'

Oh, it's roaming in the gloaming
    When the birds have gone to roost;
When the evening hate's beginning,
    And machine guns do a boost.
When you're crawling on the ground,
    While the bullets flick around,
Oh! It's very jolly roaming in the gloaming.

Just roaming in the gloaming
    When the flares drop on your head,
And you wonder if your friends at home
    Will know that you are dead;
When before your straining eyes
    Countless Huns appear to rise;
It's a merry business roaming in the gloaming.

Oh, it's roaming in the gloaming
    On an old decaying cow,
When your head gets in its stomach
    And you're mixed up anyhow;
When enveloped by the smell,
    You can only whisper "Hell".
It's a weary business roaming in the gloaming.

Just roaming in the gloaming
    When the rain begins to fall,
When you feel convinced you've lost your way
    And won't get home at all,
When you shiver and perspire,
    And trip over German wire,
Oh it's then you're fond of roaming in the gloaming.

Oh it's roaming in the gloaming
    When you're safely back at last,
When your sentries haven't shot you
    And the rum is flowing fast,
When you write a grand report
    Saying more than all you ought,
That's quite the best of roaming in the gloaming.

AT THE BRIGADE HORSE SHOW.

OUR MACHINE GUN'S INACTION.

The *Gazette* reflects the true spirit of those who lived and wrote in the trenches, not coloured by hindsight, dealing with everything that concerned them at the time, yet their hardships and dangers are often expressed in a humorous way:

A Perfect Nightmare

When you come to the end of a perfect day
    That you've spent in a forward post;
When you've picked the remaining chats away,
    And seen who has won the most;
Then you sit at ease and think it fine,
    Such a peaceful evening scene,
When Crump! Goes the burst of a 5.9
    In your best fly-proof latrine!

When you come to the end of a long, long trench,
    And you walk into No-Man's Land;
If your nose is assailed by a bad, bad stench,
    Why then you will understand
It's a dead, dead Bosch, and you'd better strive
    To break fresh ground instead,
For the Bosch has an evil smell alive,
    But a damn sight worse when dead!

The Route March

This route march is a blighted thing – God wot.
    The sun -
    How hot!
    No breeze!
    No pewter pot!
He is a blooming pool
    Of grease –
    "The Sarge",

And yet the fool
(He's large)
Pretends that he's not.
Not wet!
Foot-slogging over Belgian ways –
In summer blaze!
Ah! But I have a sign;
The sweat
Keeps dripping off this blessed nose of mine. F.W.H.

Cartoons by 'RAGS', alias Captain James, 4th Royal Berks
Verses by 'WOD', Captain W.O. Down, 4th Royal Berks

The Awakening (F.W.H.)

At night, in dream,
I saw those fields round home
      Agleam.
Drenched all with dew
Beneath day's newest dome
      Of gold and blue.

All night –
All night they shone for me, and then
      Came light.
And suddenly I woke, and, lovely joy!
I was at home, with the fields gold as when
      I was a boy.
....
Thus shall all men rise up at last to see
Their dearest dreams golden reality.

"Stand To" (With apologies to F.W.H.)

At dawn, half dream,
I see those fields in front,
      Like steam,
Drenched all with fog,
And start my daily hunt
      For louse and bug.

All day –
All day it hangs about, and then
      Comes night,
And in my soaking togs, I dreams enjoy.
But not at home by the fire's glow as when
      I was a boy.
....
Thus shall all Tommies rise next morn to see
Their dearest friend, pitted and all rusty.

                        K.A. Robertson

The previous two poems epitomise the spirit of the *Gazette*, serious and nostalgic as well as mocking and realistic, helping to alleviate the horrors of trench life by turning them into shared jokes. It is no use complaining; the war is something which must be endured:

War, Modern War

'Ave yer ever carried rations to the trench at dead of night,
When yer curses and yer grumbles,
Yer trips, and then yer stumbles,
And falls down in a 'eap, when a star shell shines out bright?
        That's war, modern war.

'Ave yer ever been on sentry, when the 'ours they seem like weeks?
When yer curses and yer swears,
Yer grips yer gun and stares
Out in the thick black darkness, when it's only rats that squeak?
        That's war, modern war.

'Ave yer ever been for water, when it's mor'n a mile to go,
And yer cusses and yer fumbles,
With the pump, which loudly grumbles,
And seems to tell the 'Uns yer there, and the bullets whistle low?
        That's war, modern war.

'Ave yer ever been out listening, when the night's as black as 'ell,
And yer cusses at a tree trunk,
And yer feels, well, in a blue funk,
Fer a minute, then yer laughs, and yer mates yer never tell?
        That's war, modern war.

'Ave yer ever 'eard the screaming of a shell up in the air,
And yer cusses, when it's nearer,
And nothing else seems dearer
Than yer life! She butts ahead! The devil did y'care!
        That's war, modern war.

'Ave yer been out with a party, in the dark and in the rain,
And yer cuss when, with a thud,
Yer slips 'eadlong in the mud
And yer've got another 'our to go on digging just the same?
        That's war, modern war.

    Yes! It's war, just modern war,
    When the rations yer are lugging
    And yer breaks the water jar,
    When the rats squeak in the bushes,
    And the fireworks sky 'igh rushes,
    When yer smothered up from head to toe,
    With thick, grey, slimy mud,
    When yer mate gets 'it beside yer,
    And yer splashed up with his blood.
    That's when yer know yer in it,
    And yer out to reach the limit,
    And ye'll "carry on" and win it,
    Well! That's war, just modern war.

Things we want to see

- The teeth of a biting wind
- Jockeys for the chevaux-de-frises
- The signaller who can send a barbed wire
- The 'madame' who can darn a sump-hole (We know many men who can d__n them when the lid doesn't fit)
- Leave continuous and extended
- Peace with honour and a piece on Gloucester

One anonymous contributor, apparently one of the many rats that grew fat in the trenches, wrote to the *Gazette* in appreciation, expressing surprise at the behaviour of human beings:

The Reflections of a Rat:

The human beings we call men don't seem to have much sense;
They spend most of their energy and wits and time and pence
In digging trenches in the earth and making dug-outs, too
Then wonder their new dwelling place gets like a sea of glue.

By those whose Kultur's unrefined 'tis said to be like hell.
The point of view is everything – it suits *me* very well.
Life was uncertain in the past with dogs and boys and traps,
But little skill is needed here to pick up lots of scraps.

Though meddlesome when unemployed, and not at all polite,
The men are fairly harmless now – they've got some Huns to fight;
And often have I ventured out when all was quiet and still
To find a first-class supper laid, and feasted at my will.

I think it due to age or damp – perhaps I may be wrong –
But anyway their cheese is good – the brand is extra strong.
I'm very fond of sausages, they make you sleek and fat,
Besides 'tis getting back one's own against the hated cat.

If I were a man, I would not choose to live in this queer way,
But for a rat 'tis just A.1., and so I'm glad to stay.
Some talk in hopeful strain of war and say 'twill end anon;
The point of view is everything – I hope it's going on.

A Minor Affray (excerpt)

This is the story of a minor war which took place in my dug-out between myself and Fritz. Fritz was not a Hun, but a rat – not the common grey beast of the English barn or sewer, but a real black specimen. At first I did not regard him as an enemy. He seemed mild and inclined to mind his own business – like the German before the war. I liked his sleek appearance and apparent trustfulness.

He was a bit of a gymnast too, his best performance being to crawl along between two beams in the dug-out roof which were a few inches apart. This meant that he had to do a 'split' all the way, right legs along one beam, left legs along the other. Viewed from below, it was a very remarkable effort, and the first time I saw it I applauded so vigorously that Fritz nearly fell onto my face. Also, he had a very odd habit of sneezing. I never discovered whether it was really a cold in the head – it may have been indigestion – anyway, it was a most surprising noise which amused me at first. So, in the beginning, I suffered Fritz and thought no evil of him.

Then he began to show signs of moral obliquity. One night – or rather, early morning – I woke under the impression that something was annoying me. It was true. Fritz was annoying me by dropping large lumps of the dug-out roof on my face. Even as I turned over on my back to look up, a stream of dust and earth fell accurately into my right eye. By the time I was able to see again, Fritz had taken cover, sneezing derisively. He spent the rest of my sleep in mining a large part of the dug-out wall, and pushing it out so that it fell with a thud on top of all my washing kit and an open tin of cigarettes.

After this it was clear that Fritz was at war with me. It was obvious that he was a treacherous and very malignant rat, probably of German origin, with preposterous ideas about super-rattishness. Possibly he even imagined himself to be a super-rat, impelled by a moral duty to occupy my dug-out, and force his 'Kultur' on the inferior human being he found there. At any rate, it was plain that F.M.G. (Fritz Must Go).

I considered the tactical position. I had to admit that Fritz held the offensive, and that I had been taken by surprise. On the other hand, he was the sort of overbearing, self-confident rat who would underestimate the strength of his enemy. Very likely he thought I shouldn't put up a fight at all, but just evacuate the dug-out and pay an indemnity of cheese. His conduct bore this out, for, as I was shaving, he looked out of a hole just above my head, dropped a lump of earth into my cup, sneezed loudly twice and winked. As I had a shaving brush in one hand and a razor in the other, there was nothing to be done at that moment, but, later in the day, I laid in wait for Fritz with an automatic pistol cleverly disguised as a novel. But Fritz did not show up.

During my next morning sleep, he devised a new form of attack. This was in the nature of a Zeppelin raid. Doing his famous split-crawl to a point just over my face, he dropped with a loud 'Hoch'. I confess that he shook my morale badly the first time he fetched up all standing on my nose. The next time he tried it, Fritz made a miscalculation somewhere, for he fell on my feet. I flatter myself that the counter attack was quickly and vigorously delivered. Fritz must have flown yards. The only drawback was that the mighty kick which sent him flying nearly broke all the toes of my right foot on the dug-out roof.

Things we want to know

- Who was the officer who told his men to make a noise like a piece of cheese if they wanted to catch rats?
- Who tries to catch rats with fly papers?
- Who hog-maned the Battalion postman? And what did they say when he dropped the rat?
- Who put toasted cheese on the end of his bayonet and kept the safety catch up? Did he catch anything?
- Which member of No. 5 platoon had two flares put up because he had seen two rats on the parapet?

Unpaid !

Another misery which they managed to turn into a joke was the mud! This did not only make moving around very difficult, but it was also impossible to keep dry. In one issue, one of the *'Things we want to know'* was "Who was the Private that tried to dry his socks by a candle?"

Many soldiers suffered from Trench Foot, an infection of the feet caused by standing for hours in waterlogged trenches without being able to remove wet socks or boots. If it went untreated, the foot had to be amputated, but the only treatment was to keep drying their feet and coating them with foot powder before putting on dry socks. At one period, it was a crime to get trench foot, but, under such conditions, this law really could not be enforced.

"THE SPRING OFFENSIVE."

"At Last!"

See! What is this figure from the line, tearing headstrong over the open – mad, rushing in broad daylight? No helmet, no equipment. On, on it comes, heedless of the myriad shells that are tearing up the ragged earth. Will nothing stop him? He is fast drawing closer, now he drops in a shell-hole, now up again and on. That wire! Will he ever cross it? Yes, he's through. He has stumbled. Quick! The stretcher bearers!

They are there now and have lifted him struggling onto the stretcher. How he writhes and struggles, but four hands are holding him fast, and he is borne to the road and the ambulance. "He is not hit. I cannot diagnose it," the M.O. says. "Send for the A.D.M.S." Still nothing can he find. The man is dumb. A kindly figure stayed by that bedside till the dawn began to break, when, suddenly, as the man's eyes opened, his hand shot out and clutched an empty cigarette tin near by.

"At last! At last I've found it," he stammered. "My foot powder!"

Suitable Christmas Presents (excerpt)

For the Infantry:-
1. An outfit comprising webbed feet, wings, and waterproof plumage   OR
2. Trenches complete with waterproof dug-outs, pipe drainage, sufficient revetting material and pumps.

(We must warn our readers, however, that No. 1 is probably the more easily obtainable of the two)

For the M.O.:-
A dressing station where German shells don't attend sick parade.

Mud, Mud, Mud *(apologies to Tennyson)*

Mud, mud, mud,
On the long, straight roads. Oh, Gee!
And I would that my tongue could utter
The thoughts that arise in me.

Oh, well for the General's job
That he watches us on his way!
Oh, well for the A.S.C.
As they loll in their cars all day!

And the beastly lorries go on
To their railhead miles from the trench;
But, oh, for the touch of a glass of 'beer'
And the sound of a voice – NOT French!

Mud, mud, mud,
Day after day, oh gee!
But I hope that the sight of H (*Hebuterne*)
Will never come back to me!

"Bong Jour, Alf! Have you changed your socks to-day? If not, why not?"

D. R. O. 407. TANKS

"Derelict tanks in the Divisional Area are on no account to be
tampered with."

They'll never relieve me
(to the tune of 'They wouldn't believe me')

Got the cutest little trench
With the acutest stench,
Where yer've gotta stand and freeze,
Up in water to your knees,
And in there's rats beyond belief
Growing fat on bully beef.
Oh, it certainly seems fine
Just to think you're in the line!

But when I tell them how sick of it I am
    They'll never relieve me, they'll never relieve me:
My clothes, my boots, my face, my hair
    Are in a state beyond repair,
I'm the dirtiest thing that one could see
    But when I tell them, and I'm certainly going to tell them,
That this is not what I came out to do,
    They'll never relieve me; they'll never relieve me,
But leave me here until the moon turns blue.

Got the cutest little trench,
Which we undertook to wrench
From the Alleyman one day
When the dawn was turning grey;
And we gave those Bosches hell,
So that they turned grey as well.
We were rather rough, I fear,
From Orvillers to Poseer.

For when they told us they wanted to give in,
     They couldn't deceive us, they couldn't deceive us,
And so with bombs and bayonets
     We made an end of poor old Fritz.
'Twas the bloodiest day that one could see;
     For when they told us, and they certainly tried to tell us,
That they'd surrender if we would desist,
     We wouldn't believe them, we wouldn't believe them,
But wiped them off the German Army List.

In this song, Captain W.O. Down seems to regret the brutality of this action against the enemy. Although the soldiers were ruthless in battle, the men in the trenches realised that the Huns were brave men risking their lives for their country, just like the British Tommies. They even played practical jokes on the enemy:

Chit-Chat

"Our persistent sense of humour must be a source of severe trial to the German nation. On April 1st one of our Aeroplanes appeared over the aerodrome at Lille and dropped a football. At the sight of the dark thing dropping thro' the skies, the good Germans hurried and took whatever cover they could find. Even after the bomb bounced, they were still suspicious. But how angry when they read at last on it – 'April 1st, Gott strafe England'."

In the following poem, M.L.G. writes as a German sailor, revealing his own respect and admiration for the enemy with their "spirit daring and untired":

Chorus of Deep-Sea Huns

Our Fatherland's most trusted tool
      In all these stormy days,
We closely follow – 'tis our rule –
      The underwater ways.

Our spirit daring and untired
      To hero deeds shall leap,
And fearlessly our song inspired
      Floats upwards from the deep.

Of valiant feats and bold we tell,
      Of night work fierce and black,
Of steamer's doom, and liner's knell
      And sunken fishing smack.

We cleave the water's moving wall,
      Like phantoms grim and grey;
It closes like a mighty pall
      Upon our helpless prey.

No traveller from British port
      His quest of gold can make,
But every step with peril fraught,
      Keeps him with fear a-quake.

True, many of our Sea-Huns grand –
      This has not made us wince –
Have set out from the Fatherland
      And not been heard of since.

Numbers of these, our Supermen,
    While making history,
Seem to have vanished out of ken,
    Their fate a mystery.

Yet once again with lips set hard
    And hearts with hate aglow
We go to bring, while off his guard,
    The loathèd Britain low.

Fragment of a British Tar's song in the distance

Come on! We're waiting the encore,
    We'll square up any debts;
We've spoilt your little game before,
    Here's good luck to our nets!

The Hun Chorus dies away

M.L.G.

In the Gazette, the hatred and vitriol is reserved for the 'slackers' and profiteers.

A Brick from the Editor's Pack

We welcome the suggestion made in the press the other day that all those excused from Military Service on the grounds of 'Religious' and conscientious scruples, should be then and there disenfranchised. For surely if one's country is not worth fighting for, it can hardly be worth living in. some of the boys who come back will have something to say about it *après la guerre.*

In March 1916, G.F.C. found slackers so offensive that he exclaimed that he did not even want to go on leave where he would see them in 'mufti', civilian clothes:

To Slackers

I hope I'll ne'er get leave again
To see the English flapper swain,
With trousers creased and swishy cane,
     In mufti.

When England's empire is at stake,
When brave men die for England's sake,
Why should these 'Pip-squeaks' poodleflake
     In mufti?

Lord Derby's scheme is loopholed wide
For cowards with conscience, or with pride
Of Wilson's tap, to 'scape and hide
     In mufti.

When this war's o'er, and peace has come,
For future wars let's swear it 'some'
That all shall share the 'tot of rum'
     In khaki!

No use to hang on apron strings
Or say their job's munitioning
They'll take their part in the real thing
     In khaki.

                    G.F.C.

The "Conscientious" Shirker

The Conscientious Shirker
Slanders fighting as a sin;
His duty to his King implies
His duty to his skin.

He need not be a combatant
If conscience bars the way;
And the conscience of the shirker
Is the voice of self today.

True patriots for principles
Their lives would gladly give;
The false for quibbles, creeds and qualms
Would much prefer to live.

And since the verb 'to kill' should not
Be 'actively' fulfilled,
What better could the slacker do
Than 'passively' be killed.

Some parents give their sons without
A murmur to the war;
And others give their influence
To keep them where they are.

To such it seemeth good and well
That fairest flowers should die,
While worthless weeds and noxious seeds
Should grow and fructify.

From outpost of the Empire
Troops the Anzac to the flag
And scornful wave their emu plumes
At laggards where they lag.

They know no country here below,
The Army Corps of cranks,
And reap the fruits of liberty
Without returning thanks.

For men will prate and men will preach
And prophesy and dream,
But aye there comes the vital day
When fighting is supreme.

And save for those who kept the gate
When warring heathens rage,
How few the fruits for freeman left
In freedom's heritage.

Britannia rules the guardian waves
And trusts her sailor sons,
If Jack could have his way he'd ship
The shirkers to the Hun.

(Jack?)

Things we want to know

- Is it true that the German prisoners in England refused to work side by side with the Conscientious Objectors? Did not the prisoners (German) say, "We have fought for our country, but you ___have not even done that."?

A. E. FRASER.

" Our ' Tommies ' are always cheerful."—
From the " DAILY LIAR."

Battalion Limerick

There was a C. Company swell
Who said, "What a h___ of a smell,
    But whether from drains
    Or human remains
I am really unable to tell."

A Piratical Ditty
(with apologies to Gilbert and Sullivan)

When the enterprising sniper's not a-sniping (not a-sniping)
　　And Billy's final fury has begun (à la Hun)
He loves to see the little Taube a-flying (Taube a-flying)
　　And to listen to the rattle of the gun (Maxim gum).

Chorus: When you've military duties to be done (to be done)
　　Our life in France is such a happy one (happy one).

When in our cosy bivvys we are lying (sometimes lying)
　　And we whistle comic songs when day is done (day is done),
And with periscopic glances we see if the foe advances
　　And so on till this bally war is done (war is done).

Chorus: When you've many irksome duties to be done (to be done)
　　Our Terrier's life is such a varied one (varied one).

When down to bathe through dusty lanes we're marching (we
　　　　　　　　　　　　　　　　　are marching),
　　With our packs upon our backs we curse the Hun (in the sun)
Over cobble-stones galore, with limbs jarred stiff and sore
　　And the rifle's almost like a blooming ton (like a ton)

Chorus: When all fatigues and duties soon are done (quickly done)
　　The Private's life is quite a happy one (now duty's done).

O.L.W.

A perennial complaint was the disparity between the pay earned
by the soldiers who endured such conditions and were exposed to
unspeakable danger and those whose jobs were nowhere near as
dangerous.

In one issue, the editor sarcastically observed that "The 'Tank' driver gets one shilling and one penny a day. Bad luck old chap, but you see you are much too near the Front to get six shillings a day. Besides, any old ass can drive a Tank, can't they, eh what?"

In March, 1918, the editor responded sarcastically to a 'Vote of Thanks' passed in Parliament:

A Chat from the Editor's Flea Bag

"More thanks! This time to our noble House of Commons for the vote of thanks which they have passed to the soldiers. May we, however, point out that Votes of Thanks won't end the war, and we should appreciate them as much unexpressed even if only on grounds of economy – but, after all, members must presumably do something to earn their £400 a year. £400 is twenty times the pay of a private soldier per annum. That vote of thanks was certainly worth twenty times as much to the country as 640 men who are in trenches holding the line for twenty-four hours, wasn't it?"

Sing a Song of Sixpence,

Sing a song of sixpence, married Tommy's pay,
Four-and-twenty long debates brought eighteen pence a day,
When the Tommies heard of it they all began to sing;
That's the right and proper stuff to set before the King.

The Commons in their Council House are very bright and sunny;
Munitioneers and Profiteers are making pots of money;
Poor Tommy in the trenches, dodging Fritz's hate,
Wonders when the X. Y. Z. he'll get his increased rate.

The Ballad of Army Pay

In general, if you want a man to do a dangerous job,
Say, swim the Channel, climb St. Paul's, or break into and rob
The Bank of England, why, you find his wages must be higher
Than if you merely wanted him to light the kitchen fire.
But in the British Army, it's just the other way,
And the maximum of danger means the minimum of pay.

You put some men inside a trench, and call them infantry,
And make them face ten kinds of hell, and face it cheerfully;
And live in holes like rats, with other rats, and lice, and toads,
And in their leisure time assist the R.E.s with their loads.
Then, when they've done it all, you give 'em each a bob a day!
For the maximum of danger means the minimum of pay.

We won't run down the A.S.C., nor yet the R.T.O.;
They ration and direct us on the way we've got to go.
They're very useful people, and it's pretty plain to see
We couldn't do without 'em, nor yet the A.P.C.,
But comparing risks and wages – I think they all will say
That the maximum of danger means the minimum of pay.

There are men who make munitions – and seventy bob a week;
They never see a lousy trench nor hear a big shell shriek;
And others *sing* about the war at high-class music halls
Getting heaps and heaps of money and encores from the stalls.
They 'keep the home fires burning' and bright by night and day,
While the maximum of danger means the minimum of pay.

I wonder if it's harder to make big shells at a bench,
Than to face the screaming beggars when they're crumping up
                                        a trench;

I wonder if it's harder to sing in mellow tones
Of danger, than to face it – say in a wood like Trone's.
Is discipline skilled labour, or something children play?
Should the maximum of danger mean the minimum of pay?

As F.W.H. says, they don't "run down" the men who do safer jobs
behind the Line, but they do resent the fact that these men are
better paid than the Infantry.

R.E.

We all admire the sapper,
  He is so full of brains;
He makes the most tremendous sumps
  That keep out all the rain;
And happy should I be if I
  Could find a dug-out half as dry.

He works both day and night
  With fierce and furrowed brow –
Or rather watches others work
  And tells them why and how;
And, with a muffled kind of sob,
  Gives someone else the hardest job.

The Army Service Corps

Some men I know have billets fine
And motor cars galore;
They live – Oh, miles behind the line …
The Army Service Corps.
They often go to A____s
To pass the time away;
Their life must be a constant grind
  To earn their extra pay!

Study of a Q.M. writing a treatise on how to save fat.

Battalion ABC (excerpt)

M. is our money – exactly eight bob –
Paid us on Fridays to finish this job.

N. is the nominal labouring man
Who strikes for more wages whenever he can.

O. is the output on which we depend
To bring this detestable war to an end.

P. is the pack and the pick that we carry
With hurdle and sandbag the foeman to harry.   F.W.H.

Once Bitten __

I guess I've learned a lot of things
I didn't know before,
And one at least is very plain
Which is, unless I'm quite insane,
I shan't be such a fool again
When next we go to war.

No longer shall I yearn to do
"The wounded hero" stunt.
To do my bit, of course, I'm keen,
But both from what I've heard and seen,
A lot of soft jobs lie between
The slacker and the Front,

I'd like to be an R.T.O.
At Havre or Leicester Square,
I'd be a mass of red and blue
And look as though I'd lots to do –
And then I'd have a drink or two –
'S'n awful game, la guerre!

Or perhaps I'll join the R.F.C.
And run a Kite Balloon,
And, like a great mis-shapen star,
I'll watch the Bosches from afar,
Or go to A_____ in a car
To spend the afternoon.

But yet, I shouldn't like to be
Away when foes are near,
And, after all, one's sure to find
It's really very dull behind,

And so I think I'll change my mind
And be a Field Cashier.

As D.A.D.A.D.M.S.
I think I ought to shine;
Or A.P.M. or M.L.O.
Would suit me very well, you know;
In fact, to any branch I'll go,
But not the _____ Line.

Emma Kew (alias: Lieut. Gedye)

High Intelligence Officers jumped on their bicycles and pedalled furiously miles beyond Bapaume.—*Daily Mail.*

The R.T.O.
A Play recently produced at Connemara Court, Italy

Dramatis Personae

Miss Ruby Queen
Capt. Tootsweet, O.B.E.   (New R.T.O.)
Gunner In de Pink   (R.T.O.'s orderly)
Private Rip van Winkle   (An aged soldier)

Time – The present - about dusk
Scene – Railway Station, Slapperhinge, somewhere in Flanders.

The curtain rises displaying Pink, sitting on a chair, going over his shirt and soliloquising.

Pink: 'Old soldiers never die-ee, they simply fay-eed aye-wayee.' Got 'im! (*He kills imaginary louse with hammer and shakes delousing powder over its corpse*)

(*shouting off-stage*) Hi, you there! Put it down! I said, put that engine down! We've lost things like that before. No, you can't have that lunch basket. What's that! Eaten your iron rations? You'd better 'op it before the quarter bloke 'ears you.

(*Continues soliloquy*) Yess! Horderly to the new R.T.O., that's what I ham; last one went on leave and was sent up the line. Still, I'll tell the new bloke as how he met an 'orrible end. (*He kills another chat and says to it, "You'll have to conclude a separate peace."*)

It's a cushy job being an R.T.O., though one does have the responsibility of standing the racket if trains don't go right, not as 'ow I ever seed a R.T.O. what was brought to justice, not properly anyways. Only the other day I was ....

(Enter Ruby Queen)

Ruby: Excuse me, are you the R.T.O.?

Pink: Ham hi the R.T.O.? Well, miss, hi ham and I ham not. I'm 's local beanends.

Ruby: His local what?

Pink: His local beanends, miss. I hacts for him like.

Ruby: his *locum tenens* I suppose you mean?

Pink: Ah, well, miss, have it your own way. Well he is hout, miss, at present.

Ruby: How long will he be?

Pink: Well, he might be so long, then again he might be so long. *(He indicates length with his arms.)*

Ruby: How absurd you are.

Pink: Do you know, miss, I wish I were R.T.O.?

Ruby: Well, miss, you could travel all over my railways for nought.

RTO: *(off stage)* Orderly! Orderly!

Pink: There 'e is, miss. That's 'im.

Ruby: Him! Who?

Pink: Why, the new R.T.O.

RTO: Orderly! *(crescendo)* ORDERLY! **ORDERLY!**

Pink: 'Aint 'e got a lovely voice, miss? Coming, sir, coming.

(Exit Pink and re-enters with R.T.O. and his valise)

RTO: *(pointing)* Orderly, put my valise down there.

(Exit Ruby Queen) (RTO removes his cap, mops his brow, divests himself of impedimenta, piling it up on Pink)

RTO: Tell me, Orderly, what sort of a place is this? *(WHISTLE – BANG – CRASH)*

Pink: Quiet, oh quiet, sir, very quiet! *(Frightful noise and repeated sounds of shells arriving, during which RTO and Pink duck frequently)*

RTO: D__n it, Orderly! *(mops his brow)* I thought you said this was a quiet place. Put my valise over there. *(indicates fresh position)*

Pink: *(Aside)* 'E don't seem to know what 'e do want!

RTO: Now just point out the country to me, orderly, places of interest and so forth.

Pink: Well, sir, see that mound over there, with the wooden cross on it?

RTO: *(impatiently)* Yes!

Pink: *(very slowly)* That's where we buried our last RTO.

RTO: Good Lord! How did it happen?

Pink: A shell, sir. Only a whizz-bang.

RTO: Where did it happen?

Pink: Just where you are standing, sir.

RTO: Orderly, just put this valise somewhere else.
(RTO moves to another place)

Pink: To continue, sir, look over there as far as you can.

RTO: Yes, I'm looking.

Pink: Well, look a little farther.

RTO: What do you mean, man? Do you realise to whom you are talking?

Pink: Well, sir, you see that bully beef tin?

RTO: Yes.

Pink: Well, that's the Town Hall where the Mayor lived.

RTO: Has he gone too?

Pink: Gone, sir? Why he's there now!

RTO: No, you don't understand. I mean is he living now?

Pink: I don't know, sir; 'e 'asn't come back to earth since the Beetle 'it 'im.

(Enter Ruby Queen, with a basket and a parasol)

Ruby: Good evening, can I speak to the RTO?

RTO}:   Good evening.
Pink}

Pink: *(Aside)* Just my luck.
(Pink exits, humming "après la guerre finie")

RTO: Pray be seated. *(He offers a chair)* Can I possibly be of service to you?

Ruby: I want to sell buns on your station.

RTO: What a topping idea! Of course you shall.

Ruby: And tea, to the dear boys.

RTO: Certainly, certainly. *(He sits down at the table and adopts a professional attitude.)*

Ruby: You know, I do so admire you men who rush up our troops to the front.

RTO: We rush them up all right. We rush them up. *(Enter Pink)* What do you want?

Pink: Please, sir, there's a man that wants to know what time the 2:15 train goes.

RTO: *(to Ruby)* Excuse me. *(goes to telephone and buzzes and speaks)* Hello, hello. Give me G.H.Q. *(thinks)* Hello, Duggie, is that you? *(pause)* Quite fit. *(pause)* Oh, so glad! Any luck last time? *(pause)* Yes, rather; in fact there's a charming one here now. English and all that. *(pause)* Oh bun selling, etc. etc. Cheerio! Oh, Duggie, are you there? *(buzzes)* Give me G.H.Q. again.

Oh, Duggie, sorry to trouble you. What time does the 2:15 train go? *(pause)* Quarter past two. *(pause)* Don't be funny. Very good. *(to Pink)* It goes at 4:20 today.

Pink: *(to officer off-stage)* The RTO ses as it goes at 4:20 today, but 'e isn't certain.

RTO: *(to Ruby)* There you are. That's the sort of thing they expect me to know: what time the train goes. What's my orderly for? However, these things can't interest you.

Ruby: But they do. You interest me enormously. *(RTO rises and comes and takes a seat close to Ruby)* Oh, I meant your work interests me. *(RTO looks downcast)*

RTO: Would you like to know about my work? *(Ruby nods)* Ah, yes, my work.
(Pause in which he thinks hard)
(Aside) What the dickens DO I do?
(Aloud) Um-ah-yes, of course. Well, as I was saying….

Ruby: *(Encouragingly)* Yes?

"For information & necessary action"

RTO: Well, I get up sometimes. *(Ruby looks surprised)* I mean sometimes about 10:30 a.m., and then Pink brings me my breakfast. Invaluable feller, Pink is.

Ruby: Funny name, isn't it?

RTO: Yes, his full name is In the Pink, as he always writes home 'I hope it finds you as it leaves me – in the pink'.

Ruby: I see.

RTO: Well, then, when I've dressed, about 12 noon, I go and attend to all the fellows who want to know about the leave train, and, of course, the strain is awful. At 12:30, I am quite exhausted, so I give the order to carry on, and I go to Skindle's to be refreshed.

Ruby: You poor dear. *(RTO moves his chair a little closer)*

RTO: Well, then I have to entertain hundreds of generals. *(Ruby shows interest)* For instance, yesterday I had a corps commander to lunch, and you wouldn't believe the stupid things he talked about. For instance, he said that … *(hesitation)*

Ruby: *(very encouragingly)* Yes?

RTO: *(embarrassed)* Well, I don't think I can remember it all.

Ruby: Oh do! *(simultaneously, Ruby lowers the parasol to shield them from the audience. RTO and Ruby move closer together. Laughs giggles and other sounds are heard.)*

Pink: *(enters laughing)* Excuse me, sir. *(Sudden commotion)*

RTO: Well, what is it?

Pink: There's a man here who ses as how he's been waiting years for this train.

RTO: *(to Ruby)* Impossible, my dear, I assure you. *(to Pink)* Bring him in. *(Pink exits and returns with aged soldier)*

Pink: Come along, old bluebeard.

RTO: What's your name?

A. S.:   Winkle, Private Rip Van, sir.

RTO: Date of disembarkation?

A. S.:   August 5th, 1914, sir.

RTO: Any papers?

A. S.:   Yes, sir. *(He hands over a huge bundle of A.F.s of various colours, shapes and sizes, neatly bound with red tape. RTO goes to the table to collect papers)*

RTO: These papers are in order. You will leave by the 2:15 train; report here at 3:45.   *(AS remains)*
Is it quite clear; well, what are you waiting for?

A. S.:   I'm very sorry *(breaking down),* but I have been on the R.E. dump and got no rations, so I ate my iron rations.

Pink: Blimy, you're for it!

RTO: *(Thunderstruck. He goes over to the table and produces a red volume – Manual of Military Law)*
Ah, I feared it. Here are the very words. *(Reads)* As iron rations are liable to deteriorate rapidly when unprotected damp, it is important that only such as are required for immediate use should be uncovered. Maximum penalty – death.
(He hands a revolver to Pink, bought in Padua, 80 lire, specially made to carry without inconvenience on a Sam Brown.) Take him away, orderly, you know your duty.

(Exeunt Pink and A.S. Six shots are heard in rapid succession. Pink reports each shot. "No. 1 fired, Sir. No. 2 fired. *etc.)*

Pink: *(re-entering)* Good Lord, sir, I've missed 'im, but I've got a rabbit. *(He produces a tin of Australian multiplier)*

RTO: Very good. Inform the D.G.R.E.'s unit. *(Pink still waits)* Why are you waiting?

Pink: A movement horder, sir. *(He gets a good one from the RTO, runs out, rubbing the afflicted part)*

RTO: *(to Ruby)* Well, as I was saying … *(they approach each other)*

(Pink re-enters hesitatingly, and, seeing how the land lies, rushes out again)

RTO: *(jumping up)* I hear a train coming. It's coming!

Ruby: *(rushing for basket)* It's coming!

Pink: It's going, sir.

RTO: It's going.

Ruby: It's gone.

RTO: This has been a terrible blow for me. My only train, the 2:15, has gone and never been stopped. *(He sobs and collapses onto the chair)*

——————————— **S.**

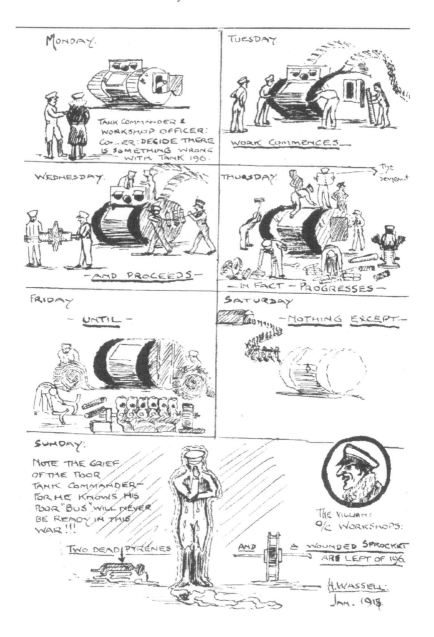

A Brick from the Editor's Pack (June 1917)

"We make no apology for quoting these lines from *Punch*. The truth which they enshrine is too often forgotten, the wrongs they reveal insufficiently realised by the people of Great Britain. The status of the Infantry man is a sad blot on our Nation's history":

For and Aft

The A.S.C.'s a nobleman, 'e rides a motor car,
'E is not forced to 'ump a pack, as we footsloggers are.
'E drives a lorry through the towns and 'alts for fags and beer,
We infantry, we does without, there ain't no shops up 'ere,
And then, for splashin' us with mud, 'e draws six bob a day,
For the further from the line you go the 'igher your rate of pay.

My shirt is rather chatty, and my socks 'ud make you larf,
It's just a week o' Sundays since they sent us for a barf,
But them that 'as the cushy jobs, they live in style and state,
With a basin in their bedrooms, and their dinners on a plate.
For 'tis a law o' nachur with the bloomin' infantry –
The nearer to the line you go, the dirtier will you be.

Blokes up at the Base, they gets their leave when they've been
          out three munse,
I 'aven't seen my wife and kids for more'n a year, not once.
The missus writes "About that pass, you'd better ask again,
I think you must 'ave been forgot." Old girl, the reason's plain,
We are the bloomin' infantry, and you must just believe
That nearer up the line you go, the less your chance of leave.

(from *'Punch'*)

Skit on the "Admiral's Song"
From "H.M.S. Pinafore"

When war broke out, I thought I could assist,
So into the Infantry I did enlist.
I finished up my training somewhere down in Kent,
And very, very quickly out to France was sent.
And the bully and the biscuits did so well for me,
That now I am the ruler of the King's Armee.

As a private in the ranks I made such a name,
That a Lance-Jack I so soon became;
I marched to the trenches with a step so light,
And I carried up the rations in the dead of night.
I went over the top so frequently
That now I am the ruler of the King's Armee.

As a Lance-Jack smart was I upon parade
That a Corporal (Full) I soon was made;
With my wiring parties always I was on 'qui vive'
That I soon had a Sergeant's stripes upon my sleeve;
And now the Sergeant's stripes did so well for me
That now I am the ruler of the King's Armee.

As a Sergeant I became so noted
To a Sergeant-Major I was soon promoted,
And then, to make a bid for popularity,
I gave away green envelopes so lavishly,
But I issued out the rum so judiciously
That now I am the ruler of the King's Armee.

As a Sergeant-Major who was known to have ambition,
The authorities were pleased to grant me a commission,

And, as leader in a bombing raid, I drove the Hun so far
That it wasn't long before I got my second star;
And from that I rose to Captain so easily
That now I am the ruler of the King's Armee.

By dodging all the work and never getting rumbled,
Into further promotion I quickly tumbled,
And the posts of Major, Colonel, General
I took in quicker time than it takes to tell,
And I 'wangled' leave perpetually
So now I am the ruler of the King's Armee.

Now, soldiers all, whoever you may be,
If you want to climb to the top of the tree,
Be advised by a soldier of the old, old school,
And you'll be a Field Marshall, if you follow this rule:
Just 'swing the lead' right lustily,
And you all will be rulers of the King's Armee.

Corporal F.O. Lyster

A Brick from the Editor's Pack

He was a Senior Officer. He had been attending a course of map-reading and had learned how to find true north from his watch. Unfortunately, a good dinner and a night's sleep drove this recondite method from his mind. Meeting the instructor the next morning, he asked him if he would mind giving him the details once more.

'Not at all, Sir, not at all. A gold watch is necessary and also a gold chain; swing the watch round the head till the chain breaks. The watch then goes west. If you then set off at an angle of ninety degrees, this will give you the true north.'

Exit the instructor at the double.

Officers are always fair game for mockery, but, even more than leaders, however, rules and regulations are a popular target for satire, especially when they don't seem to make sense in the circumstances. Some of the cartoons mocked orders from H.Q., and Captain G. Hawkins wrote these new lyrics to *'Good King Wenceslas'*:

The Yule Log

When the Captain once looked out
In comfort at Headquarters,
Where the slush lay round about,
A waste of muddy waters.
Dully shone the moon that night
And the cold was cruel,
When a private came in sight
Gathering winter fuel.

"Hither, clerk, and come to me,
If thou know'st it telling,
Yonder private who is he,
And where's his Regiment dwelling."
"Sir, he lives beyond our view
Somewhere in the trenches,
A country quite unknown to you
And full of noisome stenches."

"Bring my hat and bring my stick,
Bring my note book hither,
You and I will damn him quick,
And we shall send him thither."
Guide and Captain forth they went,
The former roused from slumber,
The latter, stern, on vengeance bent
To take his name and number.

"Have you chits for cutting wood?
Have you my permission?"
The private at attention stood
In soldierly position.
"Sir, I fear I had no leave
To gather in the timber;
No supply did I receive
From my Regiment's limber."

To Headquarters back he trod
Where the fires were burning;
Heat was in the very sod,
As he was returning.
Therefore, soldiers, now beware,
Make sure you get permission;
Always take the greatest care
To use red tape's precision.

Captain G. Hawkins

" Where IS the O.C.R.S.P.C.A. ?"

Shakespeare: 1917

Scene: A Trench. Soldiers. Night

1st Sol: *(into the darkness):* How now? Who are you?

2nd Sol: Friend

1st Sol: Pass, friend, all's well. Say now, are those the rations?

2nd Sol: No, no. The fodder will arrive apace.
E'en now they load it on the asses' backs.

1st Sol: That's bon; for I am passing fit for shackles[1]
To fill my belly to a decent stretch.

2nd Sol: And yet a mighty jest is now abroad
How shell-balls, flipping[2] round the village walls
Nigh hit the cookers, and thereat the cooks
Have scooted half way back to England's shores.

1st Sol: Ha! Ha! But halt! What's that? How now? Who's
there?

Lord I am the Earl of Monmouth, General.
Fitzjoy: Is there an officer within that trench?

1st Sol: Sir, I salute you, and will fetch him straight.

Officer: Who calls? What want you? Will you see the trench?

Lord F.: Ay, for that very purpose am I come.

Officer: Then step this way, but mind the steep approach.

Lord F.: Who's this that works not on the trench defence?
What man has dared to disobey my word?

Officer: Sir, 'tis an orderly but now arrived.
Herewith despatched from Company Headquarters.

Lord F.: 'Tis well. But mark you now my willy[3] words:
Each man shall work and dig and carry rations
Both day and night and eve and dusk and dawn.
'Tis only meet the trench should be improved.
"No dig, no dec."[4], our Lord Napoleon said,
A motto worthy of the House of Monmouth,
For like a man that hath not washed his hands
So is a man that digs not. Idleness
I must have rooted out from my command.
Slackness – the greatest enemy man has -
Is but another word for sloth, the which
I never countenance within the ranks.
But what's this here? This trench is damnable.
It badly needs both width and depth and breadth.
The wire in front is thin, the fire-steps low,
The parados still reeks of dead men's bones.
The soil is muddy – why no trench-boards down?
The grass is long and shows itself unchewed.
There's nought here schneidig[5]. You and your platoon

Officer: Methinks, my Lord, there comes a Blue Pidge[6] nigh,
'Twere best if we in yonder shelter ducked.

Lord F.: Dec me no decs – ahem ! – er – as you were!
Duck me no ducks and pigeon me no pigeons.
I will not have it said ----- *(A crash)*

Officer: Art hurt, my Lord?
'Twas nothing but a stinking neuf point deux.

Lord F.: Did it belong to us, now tell me quick,
Or came it from those baby-blasting bastards?

Officer: 'Twas theirs, my Lord.

Lord F.:   Then show me to your dug-out[7]!
(Another crash)

Officer: Look out, great Sir! They come now thick and fast,
And cert 'twas best to shelter in this cut-off[8];
The dug-out is still many paces off.
(Many crashes follow)

Lord F.: *(in the din)* The Bosch attacks – now quick – a Very
                                    Light!
Officer: 'Tis here!

Lord F.: Why don't you send it up, you wonk[9];
Send up that bloody S.O.S.[10] at once!

Officer: I wait, my Lord, until the Bosch attacks.

Lord F.: Thou ass and perisher, pass on the light!

Officer: 'Tis here. Your least desire is my behest.

Lord F.: Keep low. I'm just about to fire the charge. *(A bang)*
Oh, God! What have I done? I've shot myself.

Officer: Sire! Soldiers! Soldiers! Come around your Lord!
A sad mishap has recently o'erta'en him.

Soldiers: We're here, sir, sergeants all and stretcher bearers.

**Stretcher
Bearer:**   *(Kicks Lord F.)* Dead as a bit of bully beef entinned.

Lord F.: Villain, I am not dead, but now expire! *(Dies)*

Officer: All is now quiet without. The moon is down.
The straf is o'er. Alone the war goes on.
Bring now a blanket. I will to the phone. *(Exeunt)*

GLOSSARY

1. **'Shackles':** A dish made of bones and water, in vogue among soldiers at this time.

2. **'Flipping':** Probably refers to the shrapnel flying in all directions

3. **'Willy':** The Christian name of the then Crown Prince of Germany. Denotes here 'foolish'.

4. **'No dig, no dec.':** Dec short for decoration. No trace of this phrase can be found amongst the standard works on Napoleon.

5. **'Schneidig':** It is not clear why Shakespeare should have used the German word here. It means 'smart' or 'keen'.

6. **'Blue Pidge':** A peculiar kind of shell with feathers like a pigeon.

7. **'Dug-out':** Phatswyne-Northclieff's Dictionary for 1917 gives the following definition of dug-out – "a shelter for Cuthberts: any cover that gives protection from shell-fire."

8. **'Cut-off':** Here refers to the undercutting of trench sides, which was usually forbidden.

9. **'Wonk':** A fool.

10. **'S.O.S.':** Prbably Star of Sunset – a poetical term for Very Light. Fuller Gutz, M.A., the famous Baconian, says it should be taken in conjunction with the initial letter 'B' of the previous word 'bloody', and that it undoubtedly stood for "Bacon Shakespeare's opera scribit". I am not inclined to agree with this view.

Fibulous (alias Captain R.F. Rubinstein)

According to Shakespeare

Joining Up
Honour's thought reigns solely in the Breast. - *Henry V*

Recruit Drill
I was never so bethumped with words since I called my brother's father Dad. – *King John*

Kit Inspection
What a disgrace it is to me to take note how many pairs of silk stockings thou hast. – *Henry IV*

Sick Parade
I know a trick worth two of that – *Henry IV*

The Conscientious Objector
But for those vile guns he would himself have been a soldier. – *Henry IV*

General Inspection
And ere they be dismissed let them march by. – *Henry IV*

In France
England we love, and for that England's sake with burden of our armour here we sweat. – *King John*

Furlough
I pray thee give me leave. – *Macbeth*

Returning to France
There are other men fitter to go out than I. –*Henry IV*

-pr-s

I'd sooner live with cheese and garlic in a windmill. – *Henry VI*

Gas

If you have tears prepare to shed them now. – *Julius Caesar*

A Dud

Full of sound and fury, signifying nothing. – *Macbeth*

Sentry

Take your places and be vigilant. – *Henry VI*

After Guest Night

He arose with lank and haggard cheek. – *Lucrece*

A Blighty

And to England then,
Where ne'er from France arrived more happy men. – *Henry V*

H.Q. 6ᵗʰ Army *A.H.Q. 21-12-16*
Army Daily Orders – 21-12-16

DELIVERY TO CORPSE EXPLOITATION ESTABLISHMENTS
It has become necessary once more to lay stress on the fact that when corpses are sent to the Corpse Utilisation Establishments, returns as to the units, date of death, illness, and information as to epidemics (if any) are to be furnished at the same time.

V.S.d.O.K.   J.A. BRAUN

The Butcher: A Memory of England

1

"Any complaints?" I asked hopefully as I entered the Billet to inspect dinners.

Apparently there was a complaint.

"One at a time!" I shouted on my top G.

The musical intonation had the desired effect, and there was immediately a stony silence.

I pointed to one man who had a small, pale growth on his upper lip and was not looking quite so ferocious as the remainder.

"Well what's the m-matter?" I asked – I always stutter on m's.

For reply he pushed his plate under my nose.

"That, Sir!"

I surveyed the plate for some while, trying to recall whether it was beef or mutton night. Finally, I gave it up.

"It looks all right," I said.

"Ah, Sir, looks ain't everything!"

I could not deny this. I waited a moment.

"It's the feel, Sir. It breaks one's heart. It's so tough."

I knew what I was expected to do, but instinctively I put it off.

"Ah, perhaps it's the knives," I said, still cheerful.

"Perhaps it is and perhaps it isn't. You try and bite it, Sir," he said confidentially.

There was no hope of further respite, so I opened my mouth and prepared for the shock.

"It's splendid!" I said, a few moments later, as I vainly endeavoured to rid myself of the taste of chewed string..

Even that didn't satisfy the men.

"Oh very well," I said. "I'll speak to the Quartermaster but I m-must say I can't see anything wrong with it. It's as tender as a piece of sponge – something stuck to my throat – cake," I added. "I'd thoroughly enjoy it any day myself."

2

"Really, my dear, the m-meat seems to be getting worse and worse lately," I said to my wife a few nights later, as I fiercely grappled my way with a piece of mutton.

"I can't understand that," she replied. "The butcher's wife tells me that she's always most careful to cut off meat that she knows you'll like."

"In spite of which," I said, "it's rotten!"

Three days later the matter reached a crisis – that is to say, I lost my temper.

"Isn't there another bally butcher in the village?"

"No," replied my wife, "only Binx Brothers."

"Very well," I replied firmly. "Tomorrow afternoon we are off parade. I will go and see Mr Binx myself."

3

I had made it up with my wife before we set out the following afternoon.

"After all, perhaps you'd better do the talking. You're best at it." I had said, and, although she looked overflowing with indignation, my wife had not replied.

"Good afternoon, Mrs Paunceston," said the butcher's wife cheerfully as we entered.

"Good afternoon, Mrs Binx," replied my wife. "I've called about the meat."

"I'll just ask my husband to step up," chirped in Mrs Binx. "He's home on leave this afternoon." Whilst he was being fetched, I suddenly had a transparent flash of memory (a bad habit engendered at the cinema).

"It doesn't m-matter," I said to Mrs Binx. "Another time will do. Let's get on," I said, turning to my wife.

"Certainly not," she replied. "Why?"

"Oh, you see, I m-m-m---"

My monosyllabic monologue was cut short by the entrance of Private Binx.

"Yes, Sir?" he said, saluting me smartly, and, noticing that he had shaved off his pale moustache, I wondered why I had ever thought Private Binx had a tame countenance.

"Oh, Mr. Binx," said my wife – the irony of that civilian title! – "My husband has been complaining about the meat recently. On one or two occasions it's been quite uneatable."

"Oh, but Ma'am, that's impossible!" protested Pte. Binx.

"Impossible? But why?" asked my wife.

"Because, Madam," replied Private Binx – and here I pause to remark that Private Binx became Unpaid Lance-Corporal Binx the following day – "Because, Madam, Mr Paunceston told me himself that that meat was as tender as sponge cake, and that he thoroughly enjoyed it every day. It was meat for the million!"   A.A.A.

"SITUATION REPORT."

Enemy ration party seen on the skyline at 5-15 p.m.

"Cheero! Cook. 'Ere's another bit of meat for the stew."

Correspondence

Sir,

As you are out in France, can you tell me if we have got the Bosch in the soup? Do you think it will be all over any time now?

I am, Sir,

Yours etc.

A.S.C.

(Having studied our Cooks carefully, we should not be at all surprised at what got into the soup. As regards the latter question, from a study of the mess-waiters it certainly seems likely.)

The Canteen and Krupps

A soldier does not grow fat on army rations alone;
If he searches the dixies of shackles, he may find a hefty bone.
And when parcels are not regular and bread a loaf for three,
He tries to fit his uniform with bully beef and tea.

With prospects like those for a month, they hailed, with great delight,
The rumour passed round the trenches, "The canteen opens tonight."
The much-splashed troops poured in to spend their five franc notes,
And peaches and fags were stowed away in pockets of overcoats.

The men bought all the stuff, in unmolested peace.
The profits went up with a rush and showed a large increase,
But, within range of the German gunners, it will be clear to you
That this delightful state of things would shortly be na poo.

One day a German gunner, an evil-minded Hun,
Sighted with great accuracy and fired his blooming gun;
An eight point two came over and hit the canteen fair,
Spreading it over the landscape, with chocolate everywhere.

Oh, mourn for the pears and peaches, the Woodbines scattered about,
The cake and biscuits vanished, a fearful, bloodless rout!
Amidst the awful ruin, satisfaction was derived
And we laughed aloud at the Boche – the BEER had not arrived!

The enterprising steward was not dismayed a bit;
He sold bent tins of sausage and things not badly hit,
And now, down in the cellar, the Huns may strafe away,
He rooks each muddy soldier of all their hard-earned pay!

D.B.

Something which inspired many nostalgic poems was an idealised dream of home:

Après La Guerre

(Tune: '*Home Sweet Home*')

I dream of a time of gladness,
　　When toil and strife is o'er,
And hearts now filled with sadness
　　Will throb with joy once more.

I dream of faces beaming,
　　Of eyes, long moist with tears,
Now bright and clear and gleaming
　　With love light – Gone are fears.

Home, dearest place on earth;
　　Now, far we have wandered,
We've learned your true worth!

I dream of arms extended,
　　To welcome him so dear,
Love, joy and pride, all blended,
　　From those sweet lips, so near.

I dream, but no, I'm waking;
　　The past is gone; I'm here,
With loved ones – past all quaking,
　　I'm home. Après la guerre.

Home, dearest place on earth;
　　Now, far we have wandered,
We've learned your true worth!

G.E.K.

Nevertheless, the soldiers were often astounded, when on leave, by people's lack of understanding. One soldier, who had been sent home wounded, told of how he came out of hospital on crutches, but wearing civilian clothes. He was accosted on two separate occasions by women who challenged him because he was not in uniform! Another soldier, after seven months in the trenches, tells of how he went for a walk near his home on his first day of leave. Everything looked comfortably the same, but then he met Mrs V, who said, without listening to his attempts at replies:

On Leave (excerpt)

"So glad to see you, Arthur. How well you look! What, on leave? How nice! And when do you expect to go abroad? Soon, I suppose. I'm afraid you won't look so well after you have been in those dreadful trenches. Really, I can't think how those poor dears stand it. Fancy shells bursting all round them day and night and no pyjamas to sleep in! Well, goodbye, I hope you'll get out soon. I expect you're looking forward to it." – and off she went!

THE REAL FEELING   WHEN ON "TOUR"

Another soldier met a 'war worker', someone who claimed that she quite wore herself out 'helping soldiers on flag days:

A War Worker *(excerpt)*

"Do tell me about the war," she said. "My soldier friends tell me I know more about the war than any woman they know; but I should love to hear what you think."

And then began not so much a conversation as a parade of knowledge. It was like a catechism, save that Miss Blandish, not content with asking the questions, would not stay for an answer, but replied to them herself.

"Have you heard a shell?" she asked.

"Have you seen the Kaiser yet?"

"Aren't you glad when Sir Douglas Haig gives the word to advance?"

"Aren't you thrilled with the music of the guns?"

"When will it be over?"

"Do you have much fun in the trenches?"

"I suppose you can get leave to visit the large towns on Saturdays?"

Davin also learned that the government of the country should be handed over to the soldiers; that Mr. Asquith was a traitor; that our dug-outs were very comfy; that the Germans had no shells; that the air service was doing badly in letting us be raided; that her cousin in the motor transport was in the thick of it, and won the Military Cross on a raid; that he himself was itching to get back, and that Sinn Feiners, Conscientious Objectors, Bolos and Socialists should be burnt; that she was quite wearing herself out helping the soldiers on flag days.

Davin sat patiently and quietly while the monologue was delivered. Taking advantage of a temporary lull he rose and took his leave, regretting a wasted afternoon, but glad to meet the *couleur du rose* attitude of mind common in phlyarocratic *(nonsense speaking)* England.

A Brick from the Editor's Pack

The contempt which the so-called masters of theory have for the mere children of experience is well illustrated by the following remark addressed by a 'stay-at-home-at-all-costs' officer to a wounded officer of 16 months' experience in and in front of the FRONT LINE. "You fellows, of course, know all about how to clear up a dirty trench, but technically you know nothing at all."

No-one who had not been to war could really understand it and how it affected the soldiers. Lt. Harvey writes of the survivor guilt which will make them dread that, if they return, they will not be able to sufficiently honour the sacrifice of those who died. It is their responsibility not to let their comrades down

If We Return

"If we return, will England be
Just England still to you and me?
The place where we must earn our bread?
We, who have walked among the dead,
And watched the smile of agony,
And seen the price of Liberty,
Which we have taken carelessly
From other hands. Nay, we shall dread,
        If we return,

Dread lest we hold blood-guiltily
The things that men have died to free.
Oh, English fields shall blossom red
For all the blood that has been shed
By men whose guardians we are,
        If we return."

                                F.W.H.

HORTICULTURAL CANDOUR.

1st Tommy, to Ditto with Barrow :—

"*Wot yer doin' to-day, Jim? Carnations?*"

K. Robertson

The Fourth Commandment

Remember that thou shalt not rest on the Sabbath Day. Six days shalt thou labour and do more than thou ought to do, but the seventh day is the day of the C.R.E., and in it thou shalt do all manner of work.

The Sixth Commandment

Thou shalt kill only flies, rats, Bosch, and other vermin that dwell in dug-outs.

Lieut-Colonel (then Captain) G.F. Collett

ENGLAND AWAKES
An exaggeration in one (very short) Act

Characters
Emmy Rendle – the cook
Millie – the general housemaid
Mrs Tunnolph
Cassens – the Ration Man
A shy young girl

Scene: England   **Time: The Future**
Scene: A kitchen of a middle class house in the West End of London. Furnished in the genteel middle class way. Time (as shown by a solid kitchen clock hanging on the wall in rear) 11a.m.

On the rise of the curtain there are two occupants of the kitchen: MILLIE, the maid, seated asleep before the fire on the left in a wooden arm-chair, and RENDLE, the cook, seated at a wooden table in the rear before the window. Through the window are seen iron bars proclaiming the fact that the room is in the basement.

RENDLE is busy calculating on a slate, and, as she stops frequently to scratch her head, the calculations are evidently causing her trouble. She is a stout and plain woman of about 30. Millie is a thin and ugly girl of about 19.

Rendle: *(calculating)* One thirty-eighths, two thirty-eighths, three thirty-eighths, four thirty-eighths, six thirty-eighths … *(She pauses and looks around, and becomes aware of the sleeping MILLIE)* Drat the girl! Millie! Millie! Wake up you lazy thing.

Millie: *(Yawns and stretches herself)* Well, what is it?

Rendle: Why don't you 'elp me a bit instead of sleeping all day in front of the fire. What are seven thirty-eighths of an ounce?

Millie: 'Ow should I know? Why do you want to know?

Rendle: Silly! I'm making out our pepper allowance, of course.

Millie: I thought we was allowed a thirty-sixth of an ounce.

Rendle: So we was, but if you took an intelligent interest in the 'appenings of the day, you'd know it was reduced to a thirty-eighth of an ounce now. Yes, and 'ere's eleven o'clock gone and the ration cart due, and I ain't got 'alf my calculations done yet. Really, I don't know what things are coming to nowadays. It's enough to drive one silly 'aving to reckon out three days in advance 'ow much this and 'ow much that you're entitled to.

Millie: Well, I always sez and I always 'ave said that I think the Missus should make out them reckernings 'erself. Why, she's been to school, ain't she? And what did she learn all about them fractions for if she ain't going to use 'em now?

Rendle: Well, I call it the fault of the Government. Why do they want to give us them rations? Short of food in the country are they? Well, let the poor 'ave what there is. It won't do the rich no 'arm to go without for a change.

Millie: Lor, do talk sense Emma Rendle. Do you think the Government – the People wot gets four 'undred a year – are going to give the food to people and starve themselves? Not likely!

Rendle: I didn't say anything about wot they WAS going to do. I was talking about wot they OUGHT to do. But this chatting won't get my work done. I must get on working out these rashuns. Now, bacon. There's Master, Mistress, Miss Dorothy, yerself, myself, and the two kids. That's two, four, six, eight, ten, and two singles – that makes twelve rashers of bacon. *(She enters it on the slate)*

Millie: What yer puttin' me down for? You knows I never touch bacon.

Rendle: *(scornfully)* Silly! What difference does that make?

Millie: What about the two kids?

Rendle: They're under twelve. They're only allowed 'alf portion each.

Millie: Oh! *(There is a pause. Rendle goes on reckoning on her fingers)* I thought you said you'd put down seven thirty-eighths of pepper?

Rendle: Well?

Millie: *(triumphantly)* You're wrong! It ought to be six thirty-eighths and that ... that's three ninteenths!

Rendle: 'Ow do you make that?

Millie: There's Master and Missus – that's two, Miss Dorothy makes three; you and I make five, and the two kids – a 'alf each – makes six.

Rendle: Silly! You don't understand nothing about it. everybody, man, woman or child, hirrespective of age, is allowed a full portion of pepper, of sugar, of milk, and of salt. Of everything else, they're allowed a 'alf portion.

Millie: *(thoroughly squashed, only remarks)* Oh!

Rendle: And now don't you get worrying me again. *(She calculates for some time)* Millie, just see 'ow much jam we've got left in the cupboard, will you?

Millie: *(goes to the cupboard and opens it)* Two tins.

Rendle: We must get some more of that in from the Canteen.

Millie: Jam's awful dear now, ain't it?

Rendle: Four shillings a pound.

Millie: No, really? The Jam Manufacturers ain't 'alf got the wind up, then?

Rendle: *(thoroughly inconsistent with her former remarks)* Yes, when things 'ave come to this stage, I calls it a darn good job that the country 'as put us on rashuns. Where should we be otherwise, I should like to know?

Millie: Yes, so should I.

Rendle: It would 'ave been the food hoarders that'd have got the lot – and then they'd have been made Lords and Ladies for their services to their country. (*Decisively*) No, it wouldn't 'ave done. Wot was the good of keeping them restaurants open for the sake of the rich? Ain't Master just as well now when he takes his ration biscuit into the city, as when he used to sit for two and a 'alf hours every day over chops and steaks and I don't know what not?

Millie: 'E got a lust for blood alright through eating them biscuits, but 'e ain't so 'appy.

Rendle: (*winks*) 'E may not be as 'appy, but Missus is. That's because 'e can't waste a lot of time with the pretty waitresses.

Millie: (*jealously conscious of her own lack of beauty*) Well, it's a jolly good thing that the hussies 'ave gone into the munitions at last. It will keep 'em a bit more shut up than they used to be.

Rendle: And to think that since last Wednesday they've closed every food shop of every description. I can 'ardly credit it now.

Millie: What time is the canteen open?

Rendle: 12 – 2 and 2 - 4

Millie: I hear we're to 'ave an F.R.C. up here next week as well.

Rendle: F.R.C. What's that?

Millie: Food Reform Canteen. They're only going to sell nuts and things. It's been opened for the vegetablians and conscientious objectors.

Rendle: Well, well, I don't know what we shall be coming to next. I do believe they'll be issuing us out our rum before the war's over. *(a pause)*

Millie: Mr. Cecil hasn't been sending home so many parcels from the Front as usual lately. Why it's over a fortnight since we had the last.

Rendle: Ah yes, but it contained a fine big cake. Why that lasted them nearly a week, didn't it?

Millie: Yes, but we could do with some more soup. You can't get it for love or money now, and we're running short of sardines.

Rendle: I expect there'll be another one arriving soon. It's wonderful 'ow much food do come from the boys in France nowadays. Why, a friend of mine was telling me only the other day that ...

Millie: *(interrupting to save herself hearing a story told already half a dozen times – sarcastically)* Yes, I think it's about time that the Army in France realised there's a war on.

Rendle: *(looking out of a window)* 'Ere's Mrs Martin's maid coming down the area. I wonder what she wants. Open the door, Millie.

(Millie does so and admits a shy young girl of about 17)

Girl: Good morning, m'm. Our cook, Clara, told me to bring you round this parcel with a note. *(She puts the parcel on the table and passes the note to Rendle)*

Rendle: *(glaring)* Don't call me m'm. Call me miss.

Girl: Yes. Miss.

Rendle: Well, 'and me over the note.

Girl: Yes, Miss. *(does so)*

Rendle: *(opens the note and reads)* "Madam, Mrs Martin having informed me, her cook, that she and 'er 'usbin, the General, will be dining with your lady tonight, she 'as gave me instructions to forward you the night's rations which I herewith enclose. I beg to remain, Yours truly, Clara Alling, Cook to Mrs Martin." Oh dear, oh dear, more company! Millie, open the parcel and see what the rations are like.

(Millie opens it and produces meat, half a loaf of bread, a soup cube and four sardines)

Rendle: H'm. Not so bad. *(to the shy young girl)* Alright, missie, that will do. You can run along away home now.

Girl: Yes, Miss. *(Girl exits)*

Rendle: *(is reading the letter, suddenly calls out)* Hi! Missie! Come back a minute! Millie, call her back.

(Millie goes out and returns again in a moment with the Shy Young Girl)

Rendle: You'd better take a note with you, Missie. I'll just write one out for you. *(She gets ink, pen and paper from a drawer in the dresser, then she writes, reading aloud as she does so)* "From Emma Rendle, Cook, to Clara Alling, Cook. Parcel and contents received and noted." There! *(as she puts it in an envelope)*. Will you give that to Miss Alling with my compliments?

Girl: Yes, Miss. *(The Shy Young Girl goes out again. As she does so, she collides with an old man of about 80, who is carrying a wooden box with various things which he puts on the table)*

Rendle: Ah! The rations at last. Millie, call down Madam. *(Exit Millie)* Are they good today, Cassens?

Cassens: *(shakes his head slowly and wearily)* No. They be rotten.

Rendle: Dear, dear! What a nuisance, and company coming, too.

Cassens: You won't be feeding much company on them rations. *(He shakes his head again, sadly)*

(Enter Mrs Tunnolph, a middle-aged lady)

Mrs T.: Good morning, Mr Cassens. *(Hopefully)* Good rations today?

Cassens: 'Fraid not, m'm. Only bully beef and biscuits.

Millie: *(protesting)* That's a shame, m'm. Why Mrs Martin's just sent round some beautiful meat and …

Mrs T.:   That will do, Millie. I didn't ask for your opinion. You'd better hurry round to the canteen and get those things I told you this morning or you'll get there after it's closed.

Millie: *(meekly)* Yes, m'm. *(She goes out)*

Mrs T.:   Don't you think you could let us have a little of something else, Mr Cassens? You see, we've got some friends coming to dinner this evening. *(pleading)* Just as an exception, Mr Cassens.

Cassens: Sorry, m'm. Rations is rations. *(He takes the things out of the box as he names them and places them on the table)*

There's six tins of bully beef, four and a half pounds of biscuits with an extra quarter pound thrown in, twelve rashers of bacon, tea, sugar, pepper and salt.

Mrs T.:   Oh dear, oh dear, oh dear! What will the general say? What are we to do, Rendle?

Rendle: Lor, m'm, I don't know!

Mrs T.:   I only hope Millie's successful in getting a good supply from the canteen.

Cassens: Would you please to sign for these things, m'm, and let me 'ave any fresh ration indents as you 'ave so that I may be getting on my way again.

Mrs T.:   Have you got the indents ready, Rendle?

Rendle: Yes, m'm. It's only waiting for your signature and the dining room stamp.

(Mrs Tunnolph goes to the table and signs it, after which the cook stamps it and hands it to Mr Cassens.)

Mrs. T.:   One minute. We're going to dine with General Martin the day after tomorrow. Could we arrange to have the rations delivered straight there?

Cassens: Yes, M'm, if you give me the map reference.

Mrs. T.:   Rendle, the map!

Rendle: Here, m'm. *(She takes it from the drawer, and Mrs Tunnolph opens it out)*

Mrs T.:   *(slowly)* Let me see, it's X one four "b" – no, "c" two nine. Is that correct, cook?

Rendle: I think that X one four "c" two nine is a reference in No Man's Road, m'm.

Mrs T.:   Well, it's just by the cross roads, isn't it?

Rendle: Mrs Martin lives about three houses down in Brigade Square, m'm.

Mrs T.:   That's quite right. Then it should be X one four "d" two nine.

Rendle: That's right, m'm.

Mrs T.: Have you got that, Cassens?

Cassens: *(from behind a notebook)* Yes, m'm. Then, with your permission, I'll be getting on now, m'm. Good morning, m'm.

Mrs T.: Good morning, Cassens. *(He goes out)*

(Mrs Tunnolph, who has held up under the strain of the bad rations magnificently up till now, at length gives way to wild weeping)

(In agony) Well, Rendle, what ARE we going to do for this evening?

Rendle: I'm sure I don't know, m'm.

Mrs T.: We've got absolutely nothing else, have we?

Rendle: No, m'm, nothing.

Mrs T.: I can't understand why the food's so bad. I'm sure they must have better rations than this in Downing Street. Well, Rendle, all you can do is mix the bully beef with Mrs Martin's rations, and give us a little soup first and custard and sardines after.

Rendle: Yes, m'm.

Mrs T.: And while I think of it, Rendle. Will you tell Millie not to sound the dinner gong this evening. The General's just come back from the front and he might think it is a gas alarm.

Rendle: Yes, m'm. *(She is bending over the ration box)* Oh, m'm, here's a letter come up for you with the rations. *(She passes it to Mrs Tunnolph)*

Mrs T.: Ah, it's from Mr Cecil. *(She tears it open)* Oh no! It can't be! Rendle! Mr Cecil will be arriving home on leave at any moment!

Rendle: How wonderful, m'm!

Mrs T.: *(agitated)* Don't be silly! Don't you realise the seriousness of it? We haven't indented for any rations for him! Oh dear, oh dear, oh dear! What shall I do? Quick, Rendle, run after Millie and tell her to get all she can at the canteen.

Rendle: Yes, m'm. *(She prepares to go out just as Millie returns)*

Mrs T.: Well, Millie?

Millie: I'm sorry, m'm, but the canteen's sold out. They've nothing but cigarettes and tobacco.

Mrs T.: *(with a despairing gasp)* Oh! *(She sinks into the chair by the fire and slowly sobs. The curtain, still more slowly, descends.)*

'Fibulous' alias Captain R.F. Rubinstein

The Editor, Padre G.F. Helm, knowing that copies of the *Gazette* were read in England, took the opportunity to preach a powerful sermon to those back home:

A Brick from the Editor's Pack (March 1916)

"We are sorry to see that some discharged soldiers have already been compelled to go to the workhouse. The *Daily Mail* instanced three cases a short time ago. We look to people at home who are to 'keep the home fires burning' to see that such things are not allowed to occur.

Men who have stuck it out, have risked their lives, wrecked their constitutions, and lost their limbs because "The Hun is at the gate", scarcely deserve to be treated in this fashion.

> "In time of danger and in time of war
> God and the soldier we alike adore.
> The danger o'er, the grievance righted,
> God is forgotten, and the soldier slighted."

It is up to the people of England to create a firm public opinion on this matter. It is, after all, only fair. We are not asking you at home to send additional parcels, much as we appreciate them, but we do ask you to undertake that the maimed, the halt, the blind, the broken men, men who are perforce the flotsam and jetsam from the cruel waves of war, men who have toiled and moiled in danger that you might live in safety, and, in some cases, amass nice war profits, that these men should be cared for now that their usefulness is over and their capacity for wage-earning at a low ebb. Do not let it be said of you that you were ungrateful or that you let slip the opportunity of doing what you could for those who had done so much for you."

In this poem, F.W.H. sounds sadly disappointed that the country he loves is "austere and loveless" to its soldiers:

The Soldier Speaks

Within my heart I safely keep,
    England, what things are yours:
Your clouds, and cloud-like flocks of sheep
    That drift o'er windy moors.
Possessing nought, I proudly hold
    Great hills and little gay
Hill-towns set black on sunrise-gold
    At breaking of the day.

Though unto me you be austere
    And loveless, darling land,
Though you be cold and hard, my dear,
    And will not understand,
Yet I have fought and bled for you,
    And by that self-same sign,
Still must I love you, yearn to you,
    England – how truly mine!
                  F.W.H.

The Flag

Banner, drooping in graceful folds,
Floating or furled by the wind's caress,
What is your magic that thrills and holds
And fills our hearts with the tears that bless?
Banner, for you men have fought – and fight –
For you will die while the ages roll;
Emblem of freedom, honour, right,
Banner! You stand for a nation's soul.   M.L.G.

In August 1917, the Editor quoted a complimentary passage from
The Times and followed it with a very telling question:

A Brick from the Editor's Pack

"We owe those victories to the firm resolution of Sir Douglas
Haig, to the skilful leading of the Army Commanders and their
staffs, to the competence of subordinate leaders, to the perfect
co-operation of all arms, and, most, perhaps, of all, to the
immortal valour of our noble infantry, which continues to bear
the greatest burden in the fight, and has once more won
imperishable renown. Without it all the labours of other arms
would be in vain. It is the infantry with rifle, bomb and
bayonet that both takes and holds, endures the greatest and the
longest strain, and suffers by far the heaviest losses. Few
lookers-on witness its deeds of valour, but, if we were just, we
should distinguish its incomparable gallantry by granting it in
future the precedence over all other arms, which it has fairly
won by its devotion and its sacrifices"

At last! Then why pay the infantry less than any one else?

Fumes from the Editor's Water Bottle

Thank you, No. 15 Platoon, for letting the world know that the
following Battalions are being raised:-

    The Pawnbrokers' Battalion – they know how to
advance.
    The Shop Assistants' Battalion – they can counter-
attack, can't they?
    And, lastly, most formidable of all -- **The Boarding-
House-Keepers' Battalion** – they have learnt to charge!

TOMMY-BY-THE-WAY

Twilight. A sunken road behind the forward trenches. Above the bank may be seen the brief stems of riven trees standing gaunt against the last green daylight. They strike the note of utter desolation.

> *A Tommy enters in fighting kit. He is tired and has a guilty, haunted look. He sits down wearily and takes off his shrapnel helmet.*

Tommy: Oh my Gawd ... Oh my ... Gawd! (*He remains with his head in his hands in a torpor of despair. But it is not for long. Suddenly he looks up*)

> Why not? ... I will ... It's easy! *He jumps up, draws his bayonet and feels the point, musingly. He feels his left arm, pinching up fingers-full of muscle, looking for a fleshy part in which to make a self-inflicted wound.*

> *His hand moves up to his shoulder, and it occurs to him that just under the collar-bone would be a good spot. (Of course, it would be a very bad spot really, but Tommy does not know that.) He puts the point of the bayonet there, but his hand refuses to give the necessary push. He hesitates, looks round, picks up his rifle and fixes the bayonet.*

> *Then you realise that, amongst the enshrouding shadows is standing a Woman, for she now uncovers her face. Tall she is, mysterious you might say, for she is so dressed that her appearance suggests neither period nor age. Without further movement, she stands watching the unhappy warrior.*

He lodges the butt of his rifle against some obstacle and grasps the stock near the bayonet with both hands. With the point at his shoulder, he moves to throw his weight upon it.

The Woman takes a sudden step forward, and the soldier lets fall the rifle and turns guiltily towards her. They stand looking at one another.

Tommy: *(sheepishly)* Bonjour, madame! *(The Woman neither speaks nor moves)* Il fait chaud … beaucoup, n'est-ce-pas? Oui? *(He tries to laugh jauntily. Then, angry at her continued silence)* Oh all right! If you don't comprenny yer own blasted lingo! 'Op off, toute suite! D'yer 'ear? 'Op it! Gor blimy, why don't you learn a decent Christian language?

Woman: You poor boy!

Tommy: Oh, yer can speak English can yer? That's just like you blasted foreigners – learns our language and then looks down on us because we can't parlez-vous back. 'Spose you only learnt it so you could spy. That's wot you are, dirty lot o' spies. But you don't come spyin' on me! I ain't nothin' to do with you! Oh my Gawd! What the 'ell did I come to this bleedin' country for?
(Thoroughly wrought up as he is, he breaks down utterly and blubbers. The Woman is beside him in a minute, supporting him, and gradually his head sinks back.)

Woman: You're tired, terribly tired. A little sleep will do you good. *(She undoes the top button of his tunic. The movement rouses him.)*

Tommy: 'Ere, what yer playing at? Thought I was asleep, did yer? Was going ter see if I 'ad any despatches on me, I suppose. Well I ain't, see! But I ain't goin' to 'ave you runnin' through me pockets. I've got eight francs, and you'd like'em, wouldn't yer? I know yer! I seen your sort at the staminets.

Woman: Eight francs. They wouldn't be much use to me. I possess far, far more than that. *(She rests a hand on the rifle)*

Tommy: And I can well believe it! The profits you people make out of us is somethink wicked. 'Ere, give me that rifle! I'm off!

Woman: Have you finished cleaning it?

Tommy: What?

Woman: Weren't you cleaning it just now?

Tommy: Did it look as though I were cleanin' of it?

Woman: You had your back to me.

Tommy: J'ever see a bloke clean 'is rifle with the bayonet on?

Woman: I'm only a woman, you know.

Tommy: What's it got ter do with you any'ow?

Woman: More than you think.

Tommy: Oh, 'as it? Then if it's so important for you ter know, I'll bloomin' well tell yer. I'm fed up! I was goin' ter give myself a blighty touch.

Woman: A self-inflicted wound! Yes, I knew that!

Tommy: Then what yer want to ask for?

Woman: Because I wanted to hear you confess it.

Tommy: Oh did yer? Well if yer think yer goin' to get me shot at dawn every day for a week, yer bloomin' well mistaken, 'cos yer 'aven't got no witnesses, see!

Woman: Why are you so fed up?

Tommy: Wouldn't you be fed up if you'd gorn through what I 'ave? It's been just blinkin' 'ell for the last few weeks. Ever 'eard a shell burst?

Woman: Many thousands.

Tommy: Well, I've 'eard millions! Millions, I tell yer! And that ain't no exaggeration! I've been in trenches what's been blown ter pieces all about me, and me pals all killed or wounded.

Woman: Your pals all killed or wounded! And now you're running away. A … a …

Tommy: Go on! Say it! A coward!

Woman: Oh no! I wasn't going to say a coward. I was going to say a son of some poor mother in England who looks up to you as her hero.

Tommy: 'Ere, 'ere, come off that! I don't want none of your 'ero stuff thrown at me. I'm just an ordinary bloke, I am. I never wanted ter be no 'ero. I was earning me 25 bob a week before this blarsted war came on. A darned good job I got in them days.

Woman: And yet you gave it up.

Tommy: 'Cos why? 'Cos my girl said if I didn't chuck my job and … and …

Woman: And be a man?

Tommy: She'd chuck me.

Woman: That was the spirit of the Women of England speaking! And so you listened to her and joined up.

Tommy: Well I 'ad to, didn't I? I wasn't goin' to 'ave 'er calling me a coward! Easy enough for 'er to jaw! She 'adn't got to go through it. Didn't 'alf fancy 'erself walkin' on me arm and lookin' at other girls whose blokes wasn't in khaki!

Woman: And when you left for France there were no tears?

Tommy: Well, she laughed so as I could see she was merry and bright, but I sort of noticed she kept 'er 'ead down. And when the train moved off, she waved 'er 'andkerchief, and I snatched it for fun like, and … *(seriously)* Lor' lummy, it weren't 'alf wet!

Woman: And yet you say she didn't have to go through it?

Tommy: Oh … well … *(cheerfully)* I've got 'er 'andkerchief 'ere. *(Pulls it out)* It's dry now.

Woman: But her eyes are not. And when you go back to her and say "I ran away", do you think she'll walk with dry eyes and a smiling face down that little street in Islington?

Tommy: Oh, chuck it! *(with sudden surprise)* 'Ere, Islington! I never told you she lives at Islington!

Woman: But I knew, didn't I?

Tommy: You don't come from Islington?

Woman: I come from North, South, East and West.

Tommy: 'Ere but 'onest, do you know 'er?

Woman: I know every mother, wife, sister and sweetheart.

Tommy: Lor' lummy, you are a rum un! Who are yer?

Woman: I've been waiting for you to ask me that. I am the Spirit of the Women of England.

Tommy: The Spirit …

Woman: … of the Women of England. I was when England first was. And down through all the historied years I have watched and waited while my men made England what it is.

Tommy: 'Ere but a spirit …. That's what …. Blimy!

Woman: I know exactly. You're wondering if it's shell shock. It seems so strange, doesn't it, to see me talking to you like … like your girl might. Yet I've often talked to you before.

Tommy: You 'ave?

Woman: There was that time when you had to join up or be chucked. Of course, you didn't know it was I. Then each time letters have come from home I've been with you. And you remember that night when they were shelling that broken battered trench you had all taken so splendidly in the morning. You were sitting in a shell hole with …

Tommy: With ole Bill Hester. We was waiting for the counterattack. Gawd, wasn't they just crumpin' the stuff about!

Woman: As you sat there, you pulled a crumpled picture out of your pocket, and, though you hadn't been talking about her before, you just said "that's 'er".

Tommy: And old Bill give a start and said "Lummy, I were thinkin' of my missus too."

Woman: Yes, I was with you both that night, nerving you, bidding you both be strong.

Tommy: Old Bill bagged nine of 'em afore they did 'im in.

Woman: You did well that night, too.

Tommy: *(modestly)* Oh, I – I nicked a few of 'em. *(excitedly)* But we 'eld that blinkin' streak o' mud, didn't we? They never retook a yard of it!

Woman: Yes, the Spirit of the Women of England was proud of her men that night.

Tommy: We was as cocky as a lot o' sparrers when we come out. *(seriously)* But, by Gawd, you should have seen them as didn't come out no more.

Woman: I saw them, for I am with every man in his last hour of pain when he lies wounded and there be none to hear his call. And, as there comes upon him the horror of a great darkness, he feels that I am at his side and Peace falls round him like a veil. And after, when the tidings come, wife, mother, sweetheart hear my voice and clutch at comfort, saying with me, "He died magnificently." Oh, if you men would only be sure of the Spirit of the Women of England, there would never be sad faces when you think of home. They are so sure of you, so generous of all they hold most dear, so certain that, come what may, their men will never fail them.

Tommy: That's all very well, but they don't know what war is! There ain't no chance for a man at all. It's all machinery and shrapnel and high explosive. What I want to know is why the 'ell … *(feeling he is talking to a lady)* s'pose I didn't oughter say that to you.

Woman: Oh yes, talk to me just like you'd talk to 'er.

Tommy: Well, why the 'ell should we be doin' it at all?

Woman: If a man insulted your girl, what would you do?

Tommy: *(indignant)* Search me! What d'yer think I'd do? *(Business of having a scrap)* Not 'arf I wouldn't!

Woman: Do you remember once when that really did happen?

Tommy: *(jauntily)* it's 'appened once or twice.

Woman: Yes, but on this particular occasion the man hit you a bit hard and you chucked it up.

Tommy: It's a lie! I never! Who told yer that?

Woman: I saw it myself.

Tommy: I tell yer it's a lie!

Woman: Oh no, it's not. It happened just now. When you were …. cleaning your rifle.

Tommy: Oh come! But that … I ain't fighting for me girl.

Woman: You're fighting for England. England's a woman you know. England is just every man's girl.

Tommy: Oh, damn England!

Woman: Certainly, if you like. You've probably "damned" your girl often enough, but it doesn't make you love her any the less. That's what our enemies could never understand. They thought because we went about and "damned" our England, we wouldn't fight for her. But we did.

Tommy: Rather! There ain't no foreigners going to come it over us!

Woman: Unless they hit a bit too hard and …

Tommy: *(remembering)* Yes, you've got me there all right! *(full of a bitter abuse of himself)* Gawd, and you said their men never failed 'em!

Woman: Oh. You hadn't failed us then. It was your hour of agony in the garden.

Tommy: I was goin' to do it! If you 'adn't just … I'd 'a done it!

Woman: I wonder. If you can hear my voice now, I don't think you would have failed us then.

Tommy: What am I to do?

Woman: Go back the way you came.

Tommy: But I can't! I ran away …

Woman: No, you only lost direction. Anyone can lose direction in the dark, and yours was a very dark hour.

Tommy: I can't go back! I could never forget I'd been a coward.

Woman: I've known those who thought they were cowards once and have afterwards shown themselves such men that they have won the Cross.

Tommy: Oh, I don't want none of yer V.C.s. Any man what's been through it knows the rot of that sort o' thing. Pictures in the papers, and girls kissin' yer!

Woman: That's only one side of it. Think of all your pals who have fallen and now lie sleeping in a corner of the field they won, with forests of little wooden crosses standing sentinel above them. Wouldn't it be worth while to wear a cross in memory of the splendid dead?

Tommy: *(awe-struck at the idea)* In memory…That would be…

Woman: Yes, wouldn't it? *(She makes passes with her hands. Sleep begins to overcome the Tommy)*

Tommy: Phew! I'm sleepy … In memory … ole Bill … lots of 'em … *(He has settled down to sleep)*

Woman: *(holding his rifle like a sentry)* Sleep and gather strength from me, the Spirit of the Women of England, who has kept vigil throughout all time. Never in any season has my nation's sword been drawn but I have been there too. Behind the path of the invader, I have wept over desolate hearths, and I have stood behind defeat to nerve the arm to victory. I have sailed in oaken ships to the outpost of the world, and in ships of steel I have kept the gates of commerce clear.

Little by little, England has given place to Empire, and I girdle the great round world across the Seven Seas. There is no land but knows me. I have strengthened the arm of the pioneer when he hewed his way through unadventured forests and harnessed the forces of nature to his will in each wild continent. Time was when I could be none other than a force behind my men, but in these later days I have a further part.

Now it is given to me to work with my hands in field and factory, in camp and hospital, and bear the physical burden of each day. Oh women of England and of our Empire, in this your greatest hour look upon me who am but a reflection of yourselves. No little thing am I, but life and love, urging, guiding, compelling, seldom with glamour, but always in great moments of trial and sorrow, and so, until the world's end, a force unconquerable.

(The Tommy stretches himself and wakes and looks around)

Tommy: Blimey, been asleep 'ave I ? 'Ello, you still 'ere?

Woman: Yes, I've been looking after your rifle. You were cleaning it when you fell asleep.

Tommy: *(hotly)* Yes! I were cleanin' it! Don't you go for to say I wasn't!

Woman: You still think I want to get you a Court Martial?

Tommy: I dunno. I s'pose not ... *(laughing queerly)* I've 'ad an awful rummy dream about you. You wouldn't 'arf laugh if I told you. Strite I dreamt you was ... never mind! But it weren't 'arf rummy. Well, I must 'op it.

Woman: You don't still think I'm a spy?

Tommy: Oh, I was a bit narked then. 'Sides ... seems sort o' sloppy I know, but ...

Woman: Well?

Tommy: You sort o' remind me of my girl. That's why I'm going to let you into a secret. Tonight there's goin' to be the biggest scrap you ever 'eard of. Them 'Uns is just about goin' to get it in the neck, and I'm goin' to be one of those what gives 'em 'ell. So long!

(He goes off singing some popular song of the moment, the Woman remains centre, her arms extended. Finally she sinks down as though in prayer, and still you hear the song of the Tommy going forward.)

Capt. W.O. Down

Tommy-by-the-Way certainly achieved the aim of boosting morale, but it also gives a very sympathetic and understanding portrayal of a soldier who has been pushed too far. It achieves even greater poignancy when we realise that Captain W.O. Down, MC, was killed in action just three months after it was printed. He acknowledged that all soldiers knew and understood the "hour of agony in the garden". They had been there; they would not judge their comrades for a temporary lapse into despair.

Woodbine Willie (Padre G. A. Studdert Kennedy, Worcestershire Regiment), who entertained the troops with his **Rough Rhymes of a Padre**, also contributed a poem, reverently comparing the sacrifices made by soldiers with the sacrifice of Jesus Christ:

Walking Wounded

Still I see them coming, coming
    In their broken ragged line,
Walking wounded in the sunlight,
    Clothed in majesty divine.
For the fairest of the lilies
    That God's summer ever sees
Ne'er was robed in royal beauty
    Such as decks the least of these;
Tattered, torn and bloody khaki,
    Gleams of white flesh in the sun,
Robes symbolic of their glory
    And the great deeds they have done:
Purple robes and snowy linen
    Have for earthly kings sufficed,
But these bloody, sweaty tatters
    Were the robes of Jesus Christ.
                    Woodbine Willie

The following prayer for comrades who died in the Battle of the Somme was printed in July, 1916. It was submitted by Lieutenant Cyril Winterbotham, killed the day after he handed in his poem.

The Cross of Wood

God be with you and us who go our way
And leave you dead upon the ground you won.
For you at last the long fatigue is done,
The harsh march ended. You have rest today.

You were our friends. With you we watched the dawn
Gleam through the rain of the long winter night;
With you we laboured till the morning light
Broke on the village, shell-destroyed and torn.

Not now for you the glorious return
To steep Stroud valleys, to the Severn leas,
By Tewkesbury and Gloucester, or the trees
Of Cheltenham under high Cotswold stern.

For you no medals such as others wear
-- A cross of bronze for those approvèd brave.
To you is given, above a shallow grave,
The wooden cross that marks you resting there.

Rest you content. More honourable by far
Than all the Orders is the Cross of Wood,
The symbol of self-sacrifice that stood
Bearing the God whose brethren you are.

Lieutenant Cyril Winterbotham

This uplifting sense of comradeship is echoed in other poems, and it helps us to understand how they managed to endure the horrors of war:

Dying in Spring

Lo, now do I behold
Sunshine and greenery
And Death together rolled
-- Yet not in mockery.

Life was a faithful Friend
Shall I make other of that dark brother
Whom God doth send?

My dear companions – you
That have been more to me
Than grief or gaiety
This sure is true –
That we shall meet once more beyond Death's door,
Again be merry friends
Where friendship never ends.

(It was a saying of Pericles the Athenian that the loss of the young men in battle was like the loss of spring to the year.)

F.W.H.

The Dead

When the long-awaited day of peace shall dawn
      And hope arise to lift a world's despair,
Among the throng whose thankful hearts upborne
      The God of Battles praise – will they be there?

To share the joy of comrades who have stood
    Staunch and unflinching through the storm and wreck
In one great, loyal, fearless brotherhood,
    And see their labour crowned – will they come back?

Unto the loved ones left who bade them go
    So bravely, and in sorrowing memory yearn
For the hushed voice, while yet with pride they glow,
    In this most solemn hour – will they return?

Ah, surely, one with us, the souls at rest
    In reverent thankfulness to Him abide
Who gave the world deliverance, and blest
    The sacred cause for which they fought and died.

M.L.G.

Friendship

True friendship is a lovely thing and rare,
Made up of understanding, mutual trust,
And sympathy, patient and sure, the rust
Of years can never touch nor time impair,
A part of our own soul, the part most fair,
For who is true unto his friendship must
Live to his highest, faithful, kind and just,
Nor fail each burden with his friend to share.
Ready to give, uncounting, of his best,
Treasure or toil, the help of hand or brain,
And if the need arise his name defend.
Whose love will meet e'en shame or sorrow's test,
Rising triumphant, nobler for the pain,
And shine more pure and bright beyond life's end.

M.L.G.

This marching song, written by F. W. Harvey, expresses the men's pride in the Regiment, popularly known as 'The Slashers':

The Slashers

O hark to 'The Slashers', O hark to the drum!
'Tis the Gloucesters a-marching, and marching they come,
From cities and fields whence their fathers went out
To meet the King's foes and to put them to rout.
Africa, Flanders and Egypt and Spain,
Giving them glory to keep without stain,
Giving them honours to bear to old England
When victory-crowned they sail homeward again.

From land of the elver, and land of the pear,
They go never grieving war's hardships to wear.
Be't vin rouge or perry, they are always merry;
They fight and they die, but they never despair.
Ever the vision of homeland they keep,
Vivid in thought, but more vivid in sleep, -
Valleys of corn where the reaper is singing,
Blue coloured Cotswold made white with its sheep.

These be the things that they fought for in Spain;
These be the things that we fight for again.
Two gallant thousand they mustered of yore;
We count our comrades ten thousand or more.
Onward, then onward till victory's won!
England shall never bow down to the Hun,
Gloucestershire, guarded of Gloucestershire's lovers,
Stands, and shall stand, while the centuries run.

F.W. H.

Lieutenant King

Glossary

Alleyman:	A slang term for a German from the French 'Allemand'
Anzac:	A.N.Z.A.C. Australian and New Zealand Army Corps
A.S.C:	The Army Service Corps for supply and transport
Barrage:	A concentration of heavy artillery fire in front of advancing or retreating troops to afford them protection.
Bivvy:	Bivouac – a makeshift tent to hold a few men
Blighty touch:	A wound sufficiently serious to take the sufferer back to England
Bolo:	A spy – after Bolo Pasha, shot for treason in 1918
Bosches:	German soldiers
Bully:	Bully-beef, tinned beef
Chat:	A louse
Chatty:	Infested with lice

Chevaux-de-frises: Obstacles composed of barbed wire or spikes attached to a wooden frame, used to block enemy advancement.

Chit: Any form of hand-written message or authorisation

Crump: The shell-burst of a 5.9 or heavier shell, sometimes used of the shell itself, and sometimes used as a verb

Cuthbert: A fit man of military age ensconced in a Government office; also, any shirker.

Dump: A place, in the open, behind the line, where all sorts of military requisites were stored.

Firestep: The step running along the forward side (the fire bay) of a trench, on which soldiers stood to keep watch or to fire

Hate: A bombardment

Hun: A German or the Germans

In the pink: In perfect health

Iron rations: Emergency rations

Kaiser Bill: Kaiser Wilhelm, Emperor of Germany

Lance-Jack: Familiar term for a Lance-Corporal, the lowest rank of N.C.O.

Mufti:

Civilian clothes

Napoo:

Finished, empty, no good any more. Corrupted from the French *Il n'y en a plus* = there isn't any more

Neuf point deux:

A Nine-Point-Two: a German heavy gun much feared for the noise and destructiveness of its shell-burst.

Parados:

The rear-side of the trench was known as the parados. Both the parados and the parapet (the side of the trench facing the enemy) were protected by two or three feet of sandbags. The parados was built higher than the parapet so that the defenders were not outlined against the sky and therefore easy targets for the German snipers.

Pipsqueak:

A shell from a small trench gun

Poodleflaker:

An officer who is too willing to take part in the social side of military life

R.F.A.:

Royal Field Artillery

R.T.O.:

Railway Transport Officer

Sam Browne:

Officers' (field-service) belt with shoulder strap.

Skindles:

A restaurant at Poperinghe in Flanders frequented by officers

Strafe:	Used as a noun or a verb to refer to a punishment or telling off. Also used for a bombardment by shells. From the German phrase 'Gott strafe England' from the German Lissauer's *'Hymn of Hate'*
Sump:	One method of draining a trench was to dig an adjacent sump or pit, especially for the removal of liquid mud.
Swinging the lead:	Malingering or otherwise evading duty
Taube:	German for dove, so the name of a German monoplane which looked like a dove in flight
Terriers:	The Territorial Force (later called Army) of part-time volunteers who provided the first reinforcements organised in battalions and other units for the Western Front from October 1914.
Very Light:	A rocket fired from a brass pistol, used to illuminate No-Man's Land at night, to signal that a position had been captured, or to signal for help in an emergency.
Whizz-bang:	An onomatopoeic name for a light shell fired from one of the smaller field-artillery guns. Owing to the short range and low trajectory, whizz-bangs arrived as soon as they were heard.